Depression is a lens through which everything looks ugly and hopeless. But in this honest, raw account of his depression, Paul Asay reminds us that no matter how much depression distorts and discolors the world, God provides hope and beauty.

JIM DALY
President, Focus on the Family

I never fathomed a book on depression could be so funny, but Paul's *Beauty in the Browns* is the perfect blend of humor and heart. It's not only an eye-opening glimpse into the life of someone struggling with depression and anxiety, but a helpful guide as to understanding how to discover hope in the midst of feelings of hopelessness.

JONATHAN MCKEE
Author of over 20 books including *If I Had a Parenting Do Over*

This is a book for anyone touched by depression. Those who battle depression will learn from someone who understands it on a very raw and personal level and be encouraged to be vulnerable and honest about their personal struggles. Their loved ones will develop empathy and learn how to be effective caregivers who communicate unconditional love and acceptance. And those of us who are mental health professionals will come face to face with the effects of depression on the heart and soul and be better equipped to support the client for whom depression is a familiar foe.

JOANNIE DEBRITO, PH.D., LCSW, LMFT
Director of Parenting and Youth, Focus on the Family

Paul Asay's searching, confessional book explores the darkness and terrors many experience in their lives and families. As reported in *The Gazette*, the daily paper where Paul and I have covered religion, many Christians would rather avoid the whole subject of depression. For those who want to understand and love people who "live in the browns," Paul's humor, hope, and practical suggestions can help.

STEVE RABEY
Journalist and author

Vulnerable. Thoughtful. Personal. Paul Asay takes us to the deep unsettling waters of depression but doesn't leave us there alone. His story lovingly confronts that happy-clappy veneer of the American church and clears space for those of us who feel the weight of darkness, depression, and mental illness, either in ourselves or in those we love. He points us to an all-knowing and all-loving God who runs to us, stoops low, and calls us beloved. Maybe it's my Enneagram 4–ness or my own battles with depression (generational and personal) that make me love this book. *Beauty in the Browns* is not a breath of fresh air; it's cross-ventilation for so many.

ERIK LØKKESMOE
President, Aspiration Entertainment

Paul Asay has written a provocative, revealing book about the subject most of us don't want to talk about, whether it is about ourselves or about others. And why is that? Because we don't want to be mislabeled as weak, or cowardly, or lazy, or fearful, or far from God. But those of us who have known this illness for many years can tell you it's not a matter of fear. It is an experience of darkness and pain that is like no other.

Along comes author and writer Paul Asay to shed real light, and compassion, on the subject. And how? By revealing his own struggle with it through a lifetime. Asay talks about the immobility of depression, the desire to lie on one's back in a bedroom, the sometimes dead end with even the best doctors and psychiatric help. So what's the answer? It's something practical, something personal, something attainable. Read about his life and discover what works for him.

JOHN SLOAN
Editor

Beauty in the Browns

BEAUTY
IN THE BROWNS

WALKING WITH CHRIST IN THE
DARKNESS OF DEPRESSION

PAUL ASAY

A Focus on the Family Resource
Published by Tyndale House Publishers

A Focus on the Family book published by Tyndale House Publishers, Carol Stream, Illinois 60188

Focus on the Family and the accompanying logo and design are federally registered trademarks of Focus on the Family, 8605 Explorer Drive, Colorado Springs, CO 80920.

TYNDALE and Tyndale's quill logo are registered trademarks of Tyndale House Ministries.

Copy editor: Julie Buscho Holmquist

Cover design by Julie Chen

Cover illustrations by Julie Chen. Copyright © Tyndale House Ministries. All rights reserved. Cover illustration of tree roots by freepik-www.freepik.com.

Author photograph taken by Ted Mehl, copyright © 2009. All rights reserved.

For information about special discounts for bulk purchases, please contact Tyndale House Publishers at csresponse@tyndale.com, or call 1-855-277-9400.

ISBN 978-1-64607-005-3

Printed in the United States of America

27 26 25 24 23 22 21
7   6   5   4   3   2   1

For Colin

CONTENTS

CHAPTER 1

HIDDEN

Deep into that darkness peering, long I stood there, wondering, fearing,
Doubting, dreaming dreams no mortal ever dared to dream before.

EDGAR ALLAN POE, *The Raven*

DEPRESSION IS FUNNY.

Not *ha-ha* funny, obviously, because it'd be super-rude to laugh at a depressed person for being depressed. It's funny in a way that might cause scientists with fake-sounding German accents to stroke their beards thoughtfully. It's funny in the same way that bologna is when it's past its expiration date, or when your dog growls at your closet door for no reason, or your football team is looking at first-and-goal and decides to punt. It's funny as in *outside the norm*, funny as in *disquieting*, funny as in *you're making me uncomfortable so please just cheer up already*.

And who could blame them? Depression is just so . . . depressing, y'know? Being around someone who's obviously depressed is not much fun. Trust me, I know: Being a person who deals with depression myself, I have days when I'd rather not hang around with me, either.

Depression's funny in that there's not much fun to be found in it for anyone. By definition, it's something of a fun squelcher. Those affected by it can have a difficult time enjoying much of anything. And like a rock chucked in the middle of a pond, the impact of depression ripples out to friends, family, coworkers, and even unsuspecting motorists and harried Starbucks baristas. Depression is a burden for those who suffer from it, a worry for friends and family, and—let's face it—a hassle for anyone else exposed to it, even in passing. In a society that doesn't dare push pause, depression is an inconvenience few can afford.

Maybe that's why so many depressed people try to hide it. If we can.

We're like vampires, only moodier.

Back in the mid-1990s, my son and I would get up every Saturday morning and, without fail, watch an animated series called *The Tick*, centered on the titular "nigh invulnerable" superhero and his accountant-turned-sidekick, Arthur. Episodes featured an array of other wacky superheroes and supervillains, some of whom would hang out for the whole show, others gone before you could blink. My favorite in the latter category? A guy in a domino mask and a caped bear outfit.

"This looks like a job for . . . Bi-Polar Bear!" he shouts. Then, crestfallen, he shakes his head. "But I just can't seem to get out of bed this month."

People not familiar with depression might imagine that the condition is just that obvious, and for some it is. No, not in terms of dressing up like a bear (though maybe a few do, and who am I to judge?), but in terms of how it impacts our waking, day-to-day realities. It renders normal life, much less the life of a superhero, impossible. It can be as obvious as Vincent van Gogh's missing ear—a debilitating sickness that cripples us, imprisons us, and robs of us of who we are and what we'd like to be.

But depression comes in many guises—seasonal to chronic, mild to severe. It dresses in so many different outfits that it might even dwarf the litany of costumed crime-fighters and evildoers in *The Tick*. And trust me, that's saying something.

Plus, frankly, there's very little money in being depressed. We gotta make a living somehow, so many of us find the energy to pull ourselves out of bed in the morning and go to work.

That's me. I hold a "regular" job, even if it's not all that regular—and even though, as my coworkers will attest, I'm not all that regular, either.

I write movie reviews for a Christian organization, so parts of the working day can feel a little like church. For instance, every Monday the ministry holds a stand-up meeting/prayer in our cavernous central hallway that we call "Main Street." These Monday-morning meetings are pretty innocuous: a joke, a prayer, ministry updates, more prayer. I typically stand on the second-floor walkway with some associates of mine, and we eye the proceedings below—applauding at the appropriate times, laughing at the appropriate punchlines, and maybe making a puckish quip or two. The idea behind these Monday Main Street stand-ups are to start the work week on the right foot: a few updates, a little encouragement, and bam! We dive into our deadlines and meetings and spreadsheets. And if some of our minds wander a bit during our gathering . . . well, that's to be expected, right? No harm done, unless you miss an announcement for an upcoming potluck.

But when my mind wanders—as it invariably does—it leaves Main Street behind and explores . . . darker avenues.

I look at Main Street below the balcony and wonder if I'd potentially die if I jumped. Likely not, so I think about hanging myself, pondering whether if I tied a rope to the railing, it'd be able to hold my weight. (I've gained a few pounds, after all.) I look at the peaked ceiling and its spiderweb of supportive struts, and I speculate how I could hang a rope up there.

These thoughts and others flow through my mind like a small, dark brook, right alongside the other thoughts I might have—the day's to-do list, past conversations, what I want for lunch. I don't touch the stream: This suicidal ideation rarely strays from its banks, and I've learned not to get too close. I don't want to die—not really. And I'd certainly not kill myself. I'd hurt too many people and miss way too many deadlines. But still, I can hear that dark stream. See it inside me. Feel it. It's run alongside me since I was twelve. Maybe earlier.

And then, someone down below says, "Oh, heavenly Father." I turn my eyes away from the beams and bow my head. I turn my attention away from death and toward God, as much as I'm able. A thread of light stitches through my darker thoughts and creates, again, the fabric of another day. "Amen." *So be it.*

And with that, the stand-up is over. I open my eyes and walk back to my desk, sharing another joke or story with a friend as I go.

Funny, right?

During those weekly stand-ups, a couple of people invariably take the microphone to tell us how we've helped people struggling with some really dark issues of their own: divorce. Infidelity. Drug use. Sexual abuse. The world is so full of hurt, and our ministry does its best to help a little. We dive into that world as best we can and write and talk and give advice and, as much we we're able, comfort. And ultimately, we want to point people toward God, where they can find the hope and healing that only He can give. He heals the brokenhearted, we read in Psalm 147, and binds up their wounds.

We're not particularly unique, and many faith-based outfits are not as office-bound as ours tends to be. Thousands of Christian ministries and organizations, and millions of Christian people, go into society's darkest corners, hoping to bring a little light to those who need it most. A 2017 study found that American households affiliated with a religion (most of which would be Christian) donate nearly $1,600 to charity every year—more than twice as much as unaffiliated households do.[1]

Contrary to what some secular observers might believe, most Christians don't live in a protective bubble of our own making, sealing ourselves away from the world's problems. We want to help. We Christians believe we have *The Answer*, and we'll yammer on to anyone who asks. It's Jesus. As silly and arrogant and Pollyannish as that may sound to some, we believe it to be true.

I've seen the power of that conviction in action. I know people who've made fortunes and spent them all in the service of God. I know people who've nearly lost their lives following Him. And then when they're out of danger, they risk those lives all over again.

Jesus loves you, we say. *He sees you. He wants to heal you and save you, if you just let Him.*

We believe it. I believe it too.

But as I listen to how God is working through our ministry to heal hurting people, I feel my own hurt inside. My emotional wounds don't feel bound. My pain does not feel salved. Sometimes, I don't feel like I've been saved. I feel as though the lifesaver missed me, and I'm still treading water. And my arms are getting tired.

Jesus is the answer. I say it. I know it. I believe it. But I don't always feel it.

Where does my salvation lie? Jesus, I know. Jesus always. But a piece of me—always small but never gone, forces my head upward—not toward heaven, but to those beams above. *Peace*, they whisper. *Escape*. And sometimes, more insidiously, *Salvation*.

Salvation. I've heard that word ever since I can remember, before I could even tie my shoes. It's a beautiful word, I think, representing a beautiful idea. To be saved. The word's related to the word *salvage*, too, which seems wholly fitting. We're broken by sin, we're taught in Sunday school on up. We're twisted and mangled by our own pettiness and selfishness and desires. By all rights, we should be tossed out with the garbage, thrown into Gehenna. The devil, as old-timey preacher Jonathan Edwards said in *Sinners in the Hands of an Angry God*, "stands waiting for them, like greedy hungry lions that see their prey, and expect to have it."[2]

But God saves us. He salvages us, broken though we are. He fixes us, heals us, and shows us a better way.

So why do some of us still feel so broken?

I think most of us probably struggle at times with the reality of our own inadequacies and sinfulness. We understand what Edwards told his (allegedly fainting) congregation nearly three centuries ago: We're fallen creatures, unworthy.

I also think that most of us feel something else, too—what seventeenth-century mathematician and philosopher Blaise Pascal called the "God-shaped vacuum" at our core. We feel incomplete, like we're missing a puzzle piece or two that would make us feel whole. Most of us look for myriad ways to fill that hole, stuffing all manner of addictions and dependencies into it, hoping to find a little peace. And even those of us who try to fill that God-shaped hole with God sometimes find it doesn't quite do the trick. We love Him and worship Him and follow Him as best we can, but temptations still whisper. Old addictions still nibble away at us. Maybe it's because we're so warped and broken that the seams don't fit as they ought. Maybe it's because none of us can be fully healed on this side of eternity. "If we find ourselves with a desire that nothing in this world can satisfy," C. S. Lewis famously said, "the most probable explanation is that we were made for another world."[3]

But for those of us who struggle with depression, that sense of separation from God is deeper (and for a few of us, the desire to leave this world is consequently stronger). Maybe, at its core, that's what depression is: We can't ever forget the vacuum. And, like vacuums do, it sucks some of the joy away that we might otherwise feel. And sometimes, that sense of being an alien in your own life is so strong, that longing for "another world" is so great, we're impatient to start the trip back.

This dynamic leaves the Christian church understandably perplexed over what to do with us depressed believers. And I totally get that. Christianity is all about finding hope in the midst of a despairing world. *Gospel* literally means good news. To be depressed in the face of that news seems not just ungrateful; it seems illogical. Some would suggest that depression is even a sin.[4] *Rejoice and be glad!* They'll quote from the Scriptures. *Have you not been listening?!*

I've heard scads of sermons and devotions imploring us to rejoice, to be glad. I've written a few myself. And again, it's absolutely true.

One of my favorite go-to verses when I'm feeling particularly anxious is John 16:33: "In this world you will have trouble," Jesus says. "But take heart! I have overcome the world" (NIV).

And here's something else encouraging: Statistics suggest that faith really can be a bulwark against depression.

A 2018 study from the University of Michigan found that Christians who are lonely are less likely to be depressed than nonaffiliated lonely hearts.[5] In 2012, another study found that folks who said religion was "highly important" to them were much less likely, over a ten-year period, to report a major depressive episode than those who didn't care much about faith.[6] Yet more studies show that suicide rates are "significantly" higher for atheists and agnostics than those who adhere to a religion.[7]

It's not because Christians are inherently happier than those outside the faith, or that we're less mindful of the world's problems. Indeed, a Christian life well-lived is, I think, often harder, what with its extra responsibilities and suspicion of some of the world's (ahem) stress-relieving pastimes. But a life of faith is a life with a built-in purpose attached to it. We know that God put us here for a reason, and knowing there's a reason for us to be here gives us a bit more resilience to put up with the world's bunkum. We believe that, whatever gunk we have to deal with today, God will redeem tomorrow—that there's a purpose to it all. And yeah, we also believe that God's looking out for us, too. "For I know the plans I have for you," He says, "plans to prosper you and not to harm you, plans to give you hope and a future" (Jeremiah 29:11, NIV).

Atheists get no such assurances. They don't pop out of the womb with a God-given purpose. They have to find their own. And, not believing in a concerned Creator and (often) embracing a morally indifferent universe, they find that purpose often defaults to squeezing all the happiness and joy out of life they can. Life becomes a more selfish pursuit. And when times get tough and they're not getting what they think they ought from it, it's easier to slip into depression and, perhaps, consider turning their cards in early.

I've heard it described as the difference between pursuing holiness and happiness. Christians don't need to feel happy all the time to feel a sense of rooted, purpose-driven joy. Purpose, even when it's hard, fosters its own sense of fulfillment.

That's all great, of course. But I think that the very sense of purpose has given rise to something strange in the church itself: a cult of happiness.

It's most obvious, I think, when I flip on Christian radio. My wife loves contemporary Christian music, so I hear a lot of it when she's driving. I get it. I'm not immune to a catchy Christian earworm, and I like the Newsboys as much as anyone.

But sometimes, Christian radio stations can make me feel like I'm trapped in Disney's It's a Small World ride, only with better percussion. So happy! So optimistic! So relentlessly, aggressively positive and chipper! Each song, taken by itself, is meant to hearten and encourage people—to lift folks up when they're feeling down, even. But thirty of them together feel like propaganda: *Be happy! No, really. Be! Happy! Or else the DJ will hunt you down!*

Christian radio is an exaggerated form of what we see in lots of corners of Christianity, especially evangelical Christianity, the tradition I'm a part of. We're optimists, we evangelicals. While Catholic sanctuaries are typically graced with the corpus of Christ, bleeding and suffering, evangelical churches are graced with an empty cross. We've scrapped the somber, soaring ceilings and dark stained glass of traditional church and built light, bright warehouses filled with stackable chairs. Forget hymns and bowed heads: We raise our hands above our heads on Sunday mornings and, in some churches, we might even dance.

And all that's great, if it's a genuine outpouring of joy for being loved by God and being saved by Jesus. But not all of us feel so joyful on Sundays. Not all of us feel like celebrating.

Historically, the Church has been a place of sanctuary for hurting souls. You'd think that, of any spot in the world, the church would be a place where people could show their real selves, where they could grapple unfiltered with their own fears and angst and pain.

But the Church, at least the evangelical church, is typically not such a place. Not on Sunday mornings. For someone to carry a cloud of gloom into such a sunny sanctuary seems ungrateful and uncouth. With every face holding a smile, we plaster on one of our own. Perhaps we raise our hands so we don't look out of place, singing joyous worship songs as we feel anything but joyful.

And so the Church, with no malice on its part, sometimes shuts down or shuts out some of the very people whom Jesus said were blessed: the poor in spirit, those who mourn. How many people come to church with a sense of obligation—a social need to pretend that everything's fine? How many of *you* do?

Christianity can indeed serve as a safeguard from depression. But no matter how much we all smile and sing, sometimes depression haunts us anyway. We may not suffer from depression at the same rates nonbelievers do, but we're hardly immune. And sometimes, it feels as though the Church doesn't know what to do with us.

Matthew Warren was the son of one of the most prominent pastors in America—Rick Warren, founder of California's Saddleback Church and author of the bestselling book *The Purpose Driven*

Life. Matthew was a committed Christian and had a strong support structure in his family. From the outside, it would seem that his life was truly, unmeasurably blessed.

On April 4, 2013—four days after Easter—he spent the evening with his mom and dad, watching television and laughing. Everything, it was said, felt pretty normal.

The next night, Rick Warren and his wife, Kay, stood outside Matthew's locked house, holding each other. He didn't come to the door when they knocked. He didn't answer when they called. They couldn't get inside—they didn't have the keys—but they knew. They knew what was waiting for them on the other side of the door.

For years, they'd known that Matthew suffered from depression and mental illness. For years, they'd try to help him battle the darkness inside him. His father said that Matthew's affliction might have, paradoxically, helped many others over the years: He seemed to have a sixth sense for the person in any given room who was hurting the most. He looked to have that purpose—that key component that helps so much with depression. But it wasn't enough.

In a CNN interview a few months later, Rick recalled what Matthew told him. "Dad, I can help a lot of other people," Rick paraphrased. "I just can't get it to work for me."[8]

On April 5, 2013, Matthew Warren took his own life. He'd given hope to others, but ran out of it for himself.

"For 27 years, I prayed every day of my life for God to heal my son's mental illness," Rick Warren said in his return to the pulpit July 27 of that year. He added, "We had the best doctors. We had the best medicine. We went to the best therapist. We had the most people praying. We have a family of deep, deep faith. It just didn't make sense."[9]

That's the thing. How can such a bad thing happen when you

know the Good News? How can we lose hope when we know the Author of it?

The Christian life is filled with paradox: We must be forever welcoming and forever vigilant—filled with justice while also filled with mercy, judicious without being judgmental. It's built on the biggest paradox imaginable, really—a death on the cross brought about new life; what looked like a crushing defeat was instead a galactic victory. Depression in Christianity is a paradox too. But even here, we see evidence that healing can paradoxically come out of the greatest of hurts.

In the wake of Matthew's suicide, the Warrens, especially Kay, have become fervent, passionate advocates for mental health. They've helped bring issues such as depression and suicide out into the open within the sometimes closed confines of evangelicalism. They're facilitating conversation—hard, honest talk—about these grave but often manageable problems. I've watched them, from afar, grieve and share their stories, giving permission for folks touched by depression—folks like me—to offer up their own.

"There are more conversations taking place, more pastors willing to preach a sermon on mental illness or suicide, and more people who are living with mental illness that are willing to tell their stories," Kay Warren told *Christianity Today*.[10] "More churchgoers are willing to say, 'This is a place where we should be showing up.'"

And as Kay knows, it's a place where lots of us already live.

In the summer of 2018, my son overdosed on cold medicine and ibuprofen. He was twenty-seven, the same age Pastor Warren's son was when he died. We didn't lose my son that day, but I'm well aware that the threat isn't behind him, or us. Depression doesn't release its grip easily.

It wasn't the first time he'd tried. Just the first time his mom and I knew about it.

Funny.

I've struggled with depression, off and on, most of my life. I knew that my son suffered from his own form of depression long before the overdose. Months before. Maybe years. He'd been seeing a counselor. He'd sometimes taken medication for it.

But I'd never talked to him about my own condition. He knew I dealt with it, but we'd never talked about it. He never asked, and I never volunteered. I didn't want to worry him, I told myself. Misery loves company, the cliché goes, and depression loves the company of misery. Best to simply allude to my struggles and then show him that it's possible to push on in spite of them without going into too much detail.

But let's not kid ourselves. I was afraid. I still am. It's so much easier to pretend. So much easier to smile when I'm supposed to.

But I'm scared of losing my son even more.

My own depression doesn't scare me anymore, but it terrifies me when I see it in my son. The helplessness of standing apart from him, of being unable to reach inside him, pull him out of himself. As a dad who's spent his whole life working and wanting for his kids to be safe and happy, I don't know if there's a worse feeling than that sense of helplessness—of standing outside that closed door without a key or crowbar.

It's my fault, I think to myself. *I wasn't kind enough. I wasn't strong enough. I wasn't honest enough. I wasn't sane enough. I passed whatever's wrong deep inside me on to him. It's my fault.*

And that's the depression talking too. The despair. The shame. That sense of self-pity and unworth.

It's telling that Edward Rochester locked his crazy wife in the attic in Charlotte Brontë's classic novel *Jane Eyre*. That's what we often do with mental illness: We lock it away. It's too uncomfortable, too dissonant, too funny to deal with openly. Better to stuff it behind a door and pretend it isn't there. Better to hope it simply goes away.

Of course, if you've read *Jane Eyre*, you know that Edward's crazy wife eventually burned Edward's house down and herself along with it.

For years—all of my adult life, and sometime before—I've kept my own personal crazy locked away, as much as I was able. I'm deeply discomforted by discomfort. I don't like for folks to fuss or fret or worry. I'm an accomplice to society's willful ignorance of depression. Even as I write this book, I secretly hope that those closest to me—my wife, my parents, my dearest friends—won't read it. I fear that anything I confess in these pages may change how they view me in a critical way; that when I tell a joke or laugh, part of them will be looking for the "depressed person" underneath, like they might a ticking bomb.

I'd insist—truthfully, I believe—that they shouldn't worry: As stubborn as it might be, my depression is milder than what many people suffer from, including my son's. Yes, I've had periods of my life when I've succumbed to a sense of hopelessness and despair (which I'll talk about later), but over the years, I've developed lots of tricks and techniques that help me keep it (mostly) under control, and you'll read about those, too. I know my triggers. I know some tricks to keep the worst of despair at bay. My depression mainly just whispers now, scratching on the wood, singing through the keyhole, reminding me that it's still there, reminding me to be ever vigilant, ever careful.

But even as I write that, I understand that depression can plot behind those locked doors. It can thrive back there, out of sight, under a haze of denial and desire for normalcy.

I'm fine, we say. *Nothing's wrong,* we say. And behind the door, depression smiles a little. Sometimes it laughs.

And then—perhaps with a start of horror, perhaps with a sigh of relief—we realize that we never locked it away at all. We locked ourselves in with it.

Depression is all about hiding ourselves. We lock ourselves in our rooms, literal or emotional. We wrap ourselves in little balls and sit in the back of our closets, curl in fetal positions, push the covers over our heads. We quit work, we avoid responsibility, we shun friends, we lose ourselves and the joy that God intended for us. We avoid life and, in some cases, we reject it outright—the glorious gift of life and love for an eternity of imagined dark, perpetual silence, cold and still. Oblivion comes not as a monster, but a mother, wrapping our souls in folds of bleak forever. Ashes to ashes, dust to dust. What was once created comes undone, becomes formless and empty. Over the surface of the deep.

Depression seeks to uncreate us.

But that's not God's desire. He does not want us to unmake ourselves, to lose ourselves in our own darkness.

Before Kay Warren left her home that fateful day—the day she knew she'd likely learn that her son was no longer alive—she consciously put a necklace on that read, "Choose Joy."

"I put it on because somewhere in the dim recesses of my frozen mind I was certain the only thing that would allow me to survive the loss of my son was what I knew and believed about God . . . and joy," she later wrote on Facebook.[11]

It's another paradox, really. To reach for joy in the shadow of death—not in some cheesy, Christianese way, but when that shadow is so dark and cold and clutching. That small act feels profound to me, and telling.

It reminded me of something I read in N. T. Wright's biography, *Paul.* The apostle, Wright says, was raised in an atmosphere of hope, even as the Jewish community was struggling for existence and self-identity in the Roman Empire.

"Hope could be, and often was, a dogged and deliberate choice when the world seemed dark," he writes. "It depended not on a feeling about the way things were or the way they were moving, but on faith, faith in the One God."[12]

"'Hope' in this sense is not a feeling," Wright adds. "It is a virtue."[13]

Hope is not a feeling. It's a virtue.

I'm writing this book for a lot of reasons. I'm writing it in the hopes of better understanding how I can help my son. I'm writing it to process and understand my own struggles with depression. I'd like to think that, by talking about it here and by sharing some of the things I use to deal with it, I can help people touched by depression themselves—those walking down the same difficult path or those walking alongside someone who is. I don't pretend to have a cure or a solution. I myself have more questions than answers.

But I do have a few, I think. And for those who like to skip to the end of books—to know how things turn out—I think the real key is found in that early Christian understanding of hope. It's not about what we feel, but what we do. We choose it. Hope is a virtue.

Ultimately, we choose to find hope in a world that sometimes seems hopeless. We choose joy in a culture that pushes us to despair. It's not easy, and sometimes we need a lot of help to make that choice. But ultimately, it's up to us. We hold the key to our own door. We just have to use it.

We like to keep things hidden. We want to be alone. But the only way through depression is together, shoulder to shoulder, hand in hand—to be honest even in the pain it brings, in the embarrassment we feel.

Depression is funny. It loves locked doors. It grows in the darkness. We need to lift the latches, open the curtains, let in a little air. Let in a little light.

CHAPTER 2

WHAT IS DEPRESSION?

The first ten million years were the worst. And the second ten million years, they were the worst too. The third ten million years I didn't enjoy at all. After that I went into a bit of a decline.

MARVIN THE ANDROID FROM DOUGLAS ADAMS'S
The Restaurant at the End of the Universe

WHAT IS A MOUNTAIN?

Easy, right? We know what a mountain is. A child of five knows what a mountain is—even if he's lived in Kansas all his life. If I look outside my window in Colorado Springs, I see dozens, and it's not like they're hard to discern. They literally stick out.

At its simplest, a mountain is just really tall dirt.

But *mountain* isn't as easy to define as you'd think.

There's no such thing as a "typical" mountain. Some explode on the surface of the earth like a pimple; others are squished out of the ground like Play-Doh through a preschooler's fingers. Mount Everest is more than 29,000 feet high. Australia's Mount Wycheproof is less than 500. Mount Fuji looks different than Denali. Technically, Hawaii's Mauna Kea is the world's tallest mountain—nearly a mile taller than Everest, in fact—but less than 14,000 feet of it sticks out above the sea. And then, there's a question of what makes a mountain at all. Why is that particular lump of dirt and rock a mountain, and not a hill? Are a mountain's qualifications different in Colorado (which has lots of big lumps of dirt) than, say, Great Britain? (Scotland's Ben Nevis is the tallest point in the UK at 4,413 feet. But if I stood in downtown Colorado Springs—which in many spots, by the way, is as flat as a dinner plate—I'd have to dig down about 2,000 feet to hit the equivalent of Ben Nevis' summit.)

There's no guarantee that even a pretty impressive peak will actually earn its mountain badge. Colorado may be officially home to fifty-three "fourteeners" (mountains that are more than 14,000 feet high).[1] But dedicated hikers argue this point with ardor, vigor, and—sometimes—weapons. Some will say we have fifty-two fourteeners. Or fifty-eight.[2] Or maybe seventy-four.[3] It all depends on how you quantify not just the peak's height, but the elevation of the land (called a saddle) between two adjacent 14,000-foot peaks. If a saddle's too high, a pair of perfectly serviceable mountains officially turns into a two-headed granite monstrosity.

And knowing what a mountain looks like doesn't do justice to the actual experience of climbing one. Most fourteeners have false summits—peaks that God seemingly created to just break hikers' hearts a little. ("What?" I've said more than once. "We're not at the top?") And even if they're fairly straightforward, getting to the top can be brutal. The higher you go, the thinner the air gets. By the time you hit timberline—the line above which trees dare not grow—your heart feels like it's as big as a cow's and seems like it's beating as fast as a chipmunk's. Your lungs expand and contract like a bullfrog throat, even though it feels like there's precious little oxygen to fill them. Your head grows lighter, your legs get heavier, and every step becomes an exercise of pure, stubborn will.

Depression's a little like a mountain. Only without the view.

Like a mountain, most of us think we know what depression looks like. And in part, most of us sorta do. But defining it gets pretty tricky pretty fast. In fact, if you ever hear someone say theatrically "I'm sooooo depressed," chances are pretty good that she isn't. The hallmark of depression isn't always feeling really sad: When it gets bad, it's about your inability to feel much of anything.

At its most basic, experts define depression through a collection of recognizable symptoms, which include:

- Feeling overly sad or irritable, especially with little or no cause.

- Losing interest in activities or hobbies that used to bring a great deal of pleasure.

- Changes in appetite: It might be a loss of appetite, leading to a great deal of weight loss. But it could also be an urge to overeat—assuaging the numbness and sadness with food.

- Losing sleep. Anywhere from 65 to 90 percent of people with major depression suffer from some form of sleep disorder.[4] And unfortunately, loss of sleep may feed that depression and other mental health disorders.

- Feeling fatigued much of the time. This, naturally, goes hand in hand with not getting enough sleep. But depressed people who do technically sleep enough often don't get quality sleep, leading to weariness throughout the day.

- A sense of guilt and/or worthlessness. Guilt, in Christian thought, isn't an inherently bad thing. Guilt can push us into important and necessary changes in our lives. But depressed people often feel a disproportionate sense of guilt over relatively minor offenses (or no offenses at all).

- Trouble concentrating or thinking clearly.

- Having suicidal thoughts or feelings or, especially, plans to do yourself in.

Every depressed person will exhibit at least some of these symptoms, but they by no means need to have them all. Not every depressed person is suicidal (thank goodness). Not everyone has trouble concentrating. Lots of depressed people lose weight, but for me, the allure of lemon meringue pie is typically too strong for that. (Curse you, variable depressive symptoms!) All these symptoms can vary in degree and intensity too. And to raise the difficulty level higher, most of those symptoms are shared by other conditions, diseases, and even personality traits.

Take, for instance, one of the telltale indications of depression: lethargy. This might be the condition's biggest calling card and one of its most crippling symptoms—and perhaps the biggest reason why depression (according to the World Health Organization) is a leading cause of disability worldwide.[5] Depressed people have a hard time getting out of bed, much less doing something meaningful with their time. "I am in that temper that if I were under Water I would, scarcely kick to come to the top," wrote Romantic-era poet John Keats.[6] In the teeth of a particularly severe depressive episode, some of the afflicted don't have the energy to eat (thus the weight loss). Taking a shower, to the depressive person, feels not just pointless, but nigh impossible. (And *shampooing*? Don't get me started.) For the depressed person, the phrase "life's burdens" feels less like a nice cliché than a literal 1970s-era Chevy that you have to carry around everywhere.

In his book *The Noonday Demon: An Atlas of Depression*, Andrew Solomon said that depression, at its worst, sapped his ability to do anything. He had no thoughts of killing himself because the act itself would have just required too much effort.[7] It's a sentiment echoed by the former TV talk show host Dick Cavett, who has struggled with depression most of his life. "Perhaps the saddest irony of depression is that suicide happens when the patient gets a little better and can again function sufficiently."[8]

But in those who suffer from a less severe case, depressive lethargy can look an awful lot like, well, just being lazy. And naturally, being lazy can be mistaken for depression. Friends and family members might not recognize the difference. I'm not sure *I* can even tell the difference at times. If I spend four hours playing a video game, am I depressed? Or am I just feeling particularly shiftless and looking for ways to avoid writing a book about depression?

The same goes for lots of the symptoms on the depressive docket: Insomnia could be a sign of depression, or it could be the result of a particularly stressful day, too much coffee, the time of year, or any number of factors. You might be depressed if you have trouble making decisions . . . or you might just be indecisive. Suicidal ideation is one of the most alarming symptoms of depression, but not every person who tries to kill him- or herself is actually depressed.

So, yeah, depression is confusing, and it comes with a host of misconceptions. So perhaps as we begin this discussion, we should not start by trying to define what depression is, but to say what it is not.

It is not ordinary sadness. Sadness is a very normal and very healthy reaction to life's pits and rinds. Oh, depressive people can be quite sad, of course, but that's not what makes them stand out. If we break up with someone or we lose out on a job we really wanted or someone lets us down, we *should* be sad about that. I can get pretty mopey even when the Denver Broncos lose a football game (though admittedly, as I write this in 2019, I'm getting more used to it all the time). But that's not depression.

It is not grief—even though grief can look very much like depression. Yes, when we grieve over the death of a parent or child or friend, we can feel that our own lives are over. We can sink into a state wherein it's almost impossible to do much of anything. And honestly, someone doesn't need to die for us to experience it. The loss of a relationship can knock us flat. The loss of a job can send us reeling. I think, in a way, we can even grieve the loss of our children when they head off to school and start their own lives.

But again, grief is normal and, in its own strange way, a gift of sorts. When we grieve, it means that we have loved. Our pain speaks to the depth of that love. And eventually, even our sadness may help to remind us how blessed we were to have them in our lives in the first place. The grieving process is a journey—not an easy one, but one that has a destination, a place where joy tempers sadness and loss, and where you can remember what was with a bittersweet fondness.

Depression can look like a Sisyphean form of grief—one in which you push through those terrible emotions but feel like you'll never push past them. It's not a trek through sadness and despondency, but a treadmill, where you're grinding through the same emotions again and again.

I like how Solomon contrasts grief and depression in *The Noonday Demon*: "Grief is a humble angel who leaves you with strong, clear thoughts and a sense of your own depth. Depression is a demon who leaves you appalled."[9]

Speaking of demons . . .

It is not sin (in itself). Some Christians believe that depression is simply a symptom of a lack of faith and God's promises. *Get right with the Lord*, they say, *and your mental angst and anguish will melt away like so much snow.* And I understand that on some level. We're a people who believe in purpose and answered prayers. It's not that we think that life will be easy. But the Bible tells us that God has given us all the tools we need to push through life's torments and trials. The pessimism that seems such an integral part of depression can feel, to some, like a rejection of that confidence. *Oh ye of little faith.*

But when we dig into the workings of the brain, we learn that depression is less about faith and more about science—even if the science itself is still unfolding.

We are creatures with wildly complicated operating systems, and a dizzying number of factors feed into this state of melancholia. Some are biological: Scientists have found, for instance, that the brain's hippocampus is smaller in some women who suffer from depression.[10] Research suggests that some depressed people may have faulty neurotransmitters—the process through which our nerve cells communicate with each other.[11] Most scientists believe that there's a genetic component at work too: "Heritability is probably 40 to 50 percent," according to an article from Stanford Medicine, "and might be higher for severe depression."[12] Past trauma, such as physical or sexual abuse, can increase the likelihood of suffering from depression. Certain medications can too. Life events can, of course, be massive triggers. But a lot of times, people can get depressed for little or no apparent reason at all.

Will scientists ever understand the brain sufficiently to define the causes of depression as definitively as they diagnose strep throat today? I doubt it. And honestly, I hope not. I like a little mystery in my life. I like the fact that each human mind is a little like a perpetually unfolding, ultimately inscrutable continent, where even those of us who live there find new hills and valleys all the time. To understand the human brain the way we might a car engine . . . well, that just seems to rob our lives of a little magic.

And it's not as if the Bible promises a life free of mental anguish if we just pray a little bit harder. Everyone from Job to Moses walks through some desperately dark times in their lives. The Psalms sometimes scream in mental anguish. And while ancient Israel didn't have a lot of qualified psychologists to diagnose the mental maladies of the poets, plenty seem to read like depression to me. Take this snippet from Psalm 88:

> I am a man who has no strength,
> like one set loose among the dead,
>   like the slain that lie in the grave,
> like those whom you remember no more,
>   for they are cut off from your hand.
> You have put me in the depths of the pit,
>   in the regions dark and deep.
> Your wrath lies heavy upon me,
>   and you overwhelm me with all your waves.

PSALM 88:4-7

The psalmist prays plenty, but still feels no relief. "Why do you hide your face from me?" he cries in verse 14. If depression is the product of too little faith, it seems like we're in fine company.

It is not a bad mood that can be cured with good intentions. In days gone by, depression might have been seen less as "mental illness" and more "mental weakness."

And while we better understand depression now, that sense of weakness still soaks into the discussion. *Feeling sad? Mopey? Cheer up. Get over yourself.*

I used to work for a professional rodeo organization, and perhaps the rodeo cowboy's philosophy can be summed up in two words: *Cowboy up.* It's a pretty good philosophy in most respects, and I think a lot of us feel that way when we're faced with someone who's depressed—and sometimes, even when we deal with it ourselves. *Cowboy up,* we think. *Get on your feet. Pull yourself together. When the going gets tough, the tough get going.* I could fill the rest of this book with well-meaning clichés, inspirational exhortations, and plain ol' kicks-in-the-keister.

But for those dealing with depression, it's not always so easy. For those convinced that the whole world is a gray, empty place, no pep talk or candy gram—no matter how peppy the talk or how candy-laden the gram—will give it the color and meaning needed.

And yet.

While depression is none of those things, it can have elements of all of these things. Sadness is often a symptom of depression. Grief can trigger depression. Our own sin can spawn feelings of worthlessness and hopelessness and separation from God—all of which can make us very depressed indeed.

And you know what else? Sometimes a candy gram or kick-in-the-keister is what we need to move forward.

What is depression? It's complicated, that's what.

Its causes are myriad and not fully understood. Its symptoms can vary wildly from person to person. While it comes in a handful of recognized types (mild to severe, episodic to chronic, seasonal, postpartum, etc.), it melds and morphs to fit each of us like its own awful glove. Typical depression? There's no such thing. It can show up in as many forms as the people who suffer from it. More, perhaps. I know that, over the years, depression has looked and felt different for me. Depression, like faith, is intensely personal. But if I dared express the condition in general terms—what it feels like—I'd agree with a comparison Andrew Solomon makes in *The Noonday Demon*: It feels like static.[13]

I grew up in a long-ago, far-away time when entertainment was a rudimentary thing, not far removed from Punch-and-Judy shows. We had television, but no streaming services to cue up, no DVR'ed episodes to fast-forward through. My parents didn't even have cable—an absence I'm still a little bitter about. No, our television had a set of rabbit ears and just a handful of local stations.* Some of those stations would come in pretty clearly. Turn the rabbit ears just so, and the reception was almost as good as you could get on cable. But when I tried to watch NBC (an ancient electronic destination called a broadcast network), the picture was always marred at least a little by static—electronic insects that would swarm and circle under the glass. Some days you could see the picture relatively clearly: The insects would blur the images a bit, pushing and pulling and muting the color in their black-and-white dance, but you could still tell what you were watching. A cat looked like a cat. A house looked like a house. You could even pick out different people.

But other days, you'd lose the picture almost entirely. You knew that something was underneath the static: You could see, however dimly, outline and shade. But was it a cat? Could it be a horse? Hard to tell. And no matter how much you turned the

---

* This is not why I'm depressed, you youngsters out there, but I understand why you might think so.

rabbit ears or thwacked the side of the TV (that really did work sometimes), the picture never got better. And even as the picture grew fainter, the sound seemed louder—a harsh hiss cutting through the dialogue and music. You had to turn the sound way up to hear the dialogue.

At its worst, that's what my depression can feel like: that channel on a bad day. Life fades under a sea of insects. The real world retreats against an assault of half-seen, mostly imagined fears and doubts, even as the noise around you grows louder. No matter how hard you try to find that picture underneath, you can't see it for the insects—or, at least, you can't see it enough for the image to mean much of anything.

But here's a funny and frightening thing. Even as depression (and its sister illness, anxiety) warps the world around you, it serves as an amplifier for all the gunk inside you. Your insecurities, your suspicions, your guilt, your pain. Tim Sanford, a counselor for Focus on the Family who's dealt with his own bouts of depression, tells me that depression never *creates* the feelings of sadness and unworthiness that are so common; it just makes them bigger and badder and nigh impossible to quiet and ignore. Imagine, for a moment, that your negative emotions and thoughts are stuffed in a closet somewhere in your psyche. Picture them as pots and pans, kazoos, maybe a drum or cymbal or two. You open the door and look at them now and again, maybe shuffling them around the closet and, if you're lucky, throwing some of them out sometimes.

Depression's the toddler who's just learned to open doors. He'll pull out all those negative feelings and play with them—tossing pot lids down the stairs, beating the drums through the halls, playing the kazoos at three in the morning. The noise is unrelenting. And if you do somehow manage to gather all those emotions, throw 'em back in the closet, and slam the door again, depression won't let the door alone.

The din inside grows as the music outside diminishes. You lose your ability to filter what's really important with the clanging, banging sound of your own anxieties and shame and sadness.

I've heard that the ability to filter is one of the secrets to our ability to live and succeed. Our environments are such rich places—so filled with countless sights and sounds and smells and sensations—that our minds are constantly winnowing down all that information into what we actually need to be aware of, what we need to know.[14] We're filtering out sensations constantly, which makes a muddy world feel clearer, more consumable, and thus more manageable. We need those filters in place to operate well. And if we lose them, we run the risk of being unable to operate at all.

I wonder if the same is true of our own thoughts and feelings, too. Perhaps to thrive, we need to filter our more negative emotions—not filter them *out*, because then we'd just have other problems, but sift and strain them to a more manageable level. Perhaps depression and anxiety is simply what we call it when those filters aren't working the way they should. We're flooded with an amplified sense of our own faults and stressors and the horror of everything. And in the wake of the flood of internal inputs—the need to swim in so many directions at once—you stop trying. You're no longer in control; your affliction controls you. You and the static you feel are indistinguishable. You see nothing. You feel nothing. You are nothing.

I've only been down that "nothing" path a couple of times in my life, but it's an interesting sensation. I remember feeling particularly anguished one night in college—pouring out my soul to my (surely bewildered) girlfriend in the car, parked by a cornfield. I can't remember exactly what was going through my mind at the time, but there was sure a lot of it: The insects were buzzing that night. Flooding. And then, suddenly, it felt like I'd gone under. I was so filled with the static and I was empty. My life seemed to drain away, like water in a tub. I felt like a hollow drum with not even enough energy to beat my skin and boom.

I didn't feel sad or angry or happy or relieved, though there was a curious, cold peace. I was a dead man blinking.

I think maybe we all feel that sense of emptiness sometimes when we're grieving a loved one or mourning a treasured relationship. We cry and wail and tear at our sackcloth and, eventually, there are no more tears. We're left cool and hard until God, in His infinite love, gives us a transfusion of humanity again.

But some people who suffer from depression can feel this way for weeks, even months. It overwhelms you and, like a giant mosquito, sucks you dry—depleting even your desire to scratch. It takes everything you are and everything you want to be, leaving you unable to give or receive, to do or even feel. The insects take over. And unless you do something, they'll pull you down . . . one way or another.

That's not my experience often. I'm one of the happier depressed people I know, in fact—a melancholy optimist. But even today, when I feel like I have some control over my darker moods, I still can feel like I'm watching that channel: that channel on a good day, admittedly, but a channel that still stirs with understated static. The joy I might otherwise feel is just a bit muted. My ability to deal with the world around me is ever so slightly impaired, requiring a bit more effort. Staring at the picture behind the insects requires more concentration. And depression runs through my psyche, beating its drum.

Depression is the microbrew of mental health: bewilderingly diverse and oddly trendy. In fact, if you look at the stats, depression is on the rise with pretty much every demographic you can think of.[15] But it does seem to visit certain types of people more than others.

It's more likely to affect women than men—twice as likely, in fact. Experts point to a variety of reasons for this gender disparity: Hormones can play a huge factor during puberty, menopause, and during and after giving birth. Women tend to deal with more inequity at work and, frankly, more work and pressure at home. Culturally, the average woman has to deal with more stress than the average man, as the women in my life often tell me. But men are also less likely to seek help for depression than women, which means they're inherently diagnosed less often.

Folks who care for others in their jobs tend to be more likely to be depressed too.[16] Nursing, teaching, social work, and caring for both youth and elderly are all on the list of most "depressing" careers (though I'd imagine that many working in those fields would also say they're among the most rewarding, too). Creative types—artists, actors, and, yes, writers—tend to experience depression at higher rates than others. In fact, according to Health.com, this is the job category most likely to be associated with major depression in men.[17]

And while depression is no discriminator, youth and the aged have some greater risk factors that can feed the condition. More than one in six teens have already experienced at least one severe mental disorder in their lives, according to the National Alliance on Mental Illness.[18] Adults aged eighteen to twenty-five reportedly think about suicide more than any other age group.[19] And while the elderly are not particularly prone to depression (in fact, many studies suggest you get happier as you age[20]), rates go up depending on how healthy they are and how isolated they feel. And because seniors are expected to slow down, depressive lethargy might go unrecognized—leading to depression that goes untreated.[21]

Location may have an impact on depression as well, as strange as that sounds. In the United States, people who live in rural environs suffer slightly more than those who live in cities.[22] (Oddly, a 2004 study found the opposite to be true in Canada.[23]) Cloudy, rainy Seattle is often said to be the suicide capital of the US, but a study published in *Social Science & Medicine* found that it wasn't even in the top ten.[24] Sunny Las Vegas tops that onerous list, followed by my home, Colorado Springs. Western and southern states seem to have higher rates of mental illness than those in the Northeast or Midwest. Six of the seven states with the country's highest suicide rates are clustered around the Rockies.[25] The outlier—Alaska—has its own fair share of mountains. Experts say that lots of factors play into why the west and south have higher rates of suicide, including regional attitudes toward mental health care and adequate access to that care. But might even altitude be a factor in depression? Some believe so.[26]

This past summer, some friends and I decided to hike Mount Quandary, one of Colorado's fifty-three, or fifty-eight, or seventy-four fourteeners. While experts consider it a fairly easy fourteener to climb, there's really no such thing. Quandary's challenge is its dramatic rise in altitude—about 7,000 feet in six miles. The grade is so steep that, in places, you're not hiking a trail: You're climbing stairs. And when you're already starting at 11,000 feet, each stair feels about two feet high.

One of the hikers was a college student, fresh back from a year at sea level in California. Most of us were huffing and puffing as we started the hike, but he was suffering more than the rest of us. About a half mile in, he sat down and stared at me with wide eyes. "Is it all like this?" he said.

Aside from all the biology and genetics and demographics of depression, there's one simple fact that makes the condition so insidious: Life is hard enough as it is, and depression makes it harder. And in the teeth of it, it seems that life and depression are one—and that as long as you have the former, you'll walk with the latter. Each step saps your strength, and you know the next step will feel heavier than the last. You struggle even to breathe. You try to enjoy the wonderful world around you, but you're so tired. So tired.

Is it all like this? You ask. And the depression whispers in your soul, *Yes. Yes it is.*

But depression, as I've learned, lies.

While scientists still study and debate the causes of depression, the condition is treatable. Just as the condition has no single cause, it has no single cure. Counseling can be incredibly helpful. (The ministry I work for, Focus on the Family, has counselors on staff able to talk with you if you call their helpline at 1-855-771-HELP.) Support groups can provide community in what can be a terribly isolating condition. Medication can be a huge tool in stilling the static—in restoring the brain's equilibrium and keeping it that way. According to the Depression and Bipolar Support Alliance, up to 80 percent of people who are treated for depression are successfully helped through a combination of medication and counseling.

But depressed people need help outside the doctor's office too. This most intimate of diseases shrinks, like a vampire exposed to a cross, from our most intimate resources: Friends. Family. Faith. These have been instrumental in helping me deal with my own issues. Because depression can sap your strength and will, sometimes you need to lean on others.

But there are limits.

At the very end of 2003's *The Lord of the Rings: The Return of the King*, Frodo Baggins and his loyal friend, Samwise Gamgee, find themselves on a mountain—the ominously and appropriately named Mount Doom. Frodo carries the Ring of Power, an incredibly evil (and slightly sentient) piece of jewelry that slowly destroys everyone who wears it. Frodo and Sam are on their way to cast it into the mountain's fires—getting rid of it forever. And Frodo, as the story's "Ring Bearer," must carry the Ring alone. But as he carries it, the Ring's original owner and maker, the terrible Sauron, seems to spiritually come ever nearer.

While I don't think anyone has ever compared the Ring to depression, its impact on Frodo feels, at times, strangely similar. Over the course of the story, that Ring has slowly sapped much of Frodo's strength and will and joy—becoming more alive than Frodo is himself. And here, on the rocky slope of Mount Doom, Frodo can no longer walk. He falls to the fire-torn ground, his face scarred and marred by grime.

Sam comes alongside and tries to encourage Frodo by reminding him about the Shire, their home—about the good, precious, beautiful things in life. The birds, the flowers, strawberries with cream.

"Do you remember the taste of strawberries?" Sam asks.

"No, Sam," Frodo answers weakly. "I don't recall the taste of food. Nor the sound of water. Or the touch of grass. [I'm] naked in the dark. There's nothing. No veil. He's with me in the wheel of fire! I can see him with my waking eyes!"

"Then let us be rid of it, once and for all," Sam says. "Come on, Mr. Frodo. I can't carry it for you—but I can carry you!"

It's a beautiful, powerful scene. And in the context of our subject, the story offers a sense of hope to those of us who are carrying our own depressing burdens. If our strength gives out, we may have people in our lives who can come alongside and lift us up—even carry us for a time.

But alas, depression isn't a metal ring we can just rip off and chuck into a volcano. If it was, this book would be a whole lot shorter. The burden we carry is inside us. And eventually, it's up to us to deal with it. No amount of counseling or medication or the support of family and friends will save us in spite of ourselves. We must find the will to do our part.

Depression is as varied as the people who have it. And, as such, the ultimate cure for depression may be just as variable. But in the following pages I'll share with you what I've experienced and what I feel I've learned.

I hope that you—those who struggle with depression, and those who care about someone who struggles with it—can find a little hope and, maybe, a little help. Or, at the very least, you'll feel less alone. I can't carry you, but we're on this mountain together.

PART I

DOWN

In which the author is born, grows up,
goes to college, gets married, has kids, and
suffers several bouts of depression.

CHAPTER 3

BELONGING

We live, as we dream—alone . . .

JOSEPH CONRAD, *Heart of Darkness*

WE BEGIN OUR JOURNEYS IN PARADISE.

We float in a cloud of amniotic fluid when we're in the womb, protected from the world outside. Oxygen-rich, nutrient-laden blood flows directly to us through the umbilical cord, giving us all that we need to breathe and grow. We can hear sounds as early as our twentieth week, and we're often soothed by the sounds around us.[1] We can hear our father talk to us and our mother sing. Studies have shown that babies, once born, are especially soothed by stories read to them in utero. But especially, they hear the insistent repetitive noise of life: the beat of a mother's heart, the breath in her lungs.

We don't see much, of course. And once we're out, none of us remember the experience.* But I feel like, for most of us, it must be a kind of Eden in there—the place between the Pishon and Gihon,

---

* Researchers and experts in prenatal care know that, even from our very earliest stages, we can suffer trauma from the outside world. But compared to what most of us experience later, it's a pretty peaceful, protected place.

where all our needs are taken care of, we're at peace and, most critically, we know we belong. We're enveloped in perfect, uncritical love.

And then God, in His boundless wisdom and grand design, kicks us out of the garden.

It had to be, of course. I've never been pregnant (as my wife often reminds me), but as nice as it might be for the baby, eternal pregnancy would be uncomfortable for mom. But it's still a shame. When we leave the walls of the womb, our troubles begin. Most of us are born squalling.

I said just a chapter ago that depression's a tricky thing to nail down. Its causes can vary widely, from past trauma to present stresses, from biochemical changes in the brain to changes in the seasons. And lots of times, depression doesn't seem to need a trigger at all. It just shows up at your door, suitcase in hand, and announces it'll be staying for a spell.

But I do wonder whether many, if not most, forms of depression are rooted in that sense of separation.

We are naturally creatures of community, of tribe. We instinctively gather in clusters. We celebrate family and hang out with friends. We go to church, attend rallies, fill stadiums,* and glory in not just what we're focusing on, but also our closeness with one another. We work with people, eat with people, laugh with people, pray with people. And I sometimes wonder if our communities are, in part, attempts to recover that pure intimacy that a secret, silent part of us never stopped longing for: a desire to return to some blessed garden, where we were wholly content and God walked with us. Our attempts at intimacy, be it physical,

---

*As long as there's not a pandemic going on.

emotional, or spiritual—in bed or over coffee, in a small group or concert hall—are earthbound echoes of a time before time, when we were truly cradled in the cup of God's hand. Just as salmon know instinctively where they were born and swim like crazy to get back there, we feel the tug of our own real home. We feel the ache of its absence throughout our lives. And maybe everything we do that *means* something reflects our drive to get back there . . . even if we don't know what "there" is.

The Bible is the story of love bisected—of people divorced from belonging. Eden's only the beginning: The whole world fragmented according to Babel, separated not just from God, but also each other. A curtain separated the Ark of the Covenant from the people of the covenant. Israel was torn apart, like a cloth, just three kings in. God's chosen were exiled from their own Promised Land—sent to live among strangers. When the Bible talks about the book's most horrific disease—leprosy—its horror comes not so much from the sickness itself, but the isolation it brings with it: "He is unclean," Leviticus 13:46 says. "He shall live alone."

In the Bible, it's pretty clear: Nothing is sadder than separation.

"The deepest need of man," writes Erich Fromm in his book *The Art of Loving*, "is the need to overcome his separateness, to leave the prison of his aloneness."[2] But in this fallen world, we all feel that prison in some respects—and, at times, we all feel it keenly. None of us have a perfect union with God or each other.

But depression brings its own unique sense of isolation with it. And sometimes, isolation brings on depression.

I belonged when I was born. I felt it every day for my first eight years.

I lived those years in Taos, New Mexico, long before most

BMW-driving tourists found it. Back then, it had two paved roads, one stoplight and about five quintillion bugs. It was almost as famous for its mud (the kind that collects on the bottom of your shoes till you're six inches taller) as its art.

But it did have plenty of art, too, and my dad was one of the guys who made it. He painted and sculpted and did both really well. But in a town where a wayward rock was bound to bounce off the heads of at least three starving artists, you needed a backup plan. So he did lots of other things too: He was a fireman and sold ads for the weekly newspaper. He drew political cartoons and taught kids art for the local elementary school. But back then, I mostly remember him as a caricaturist: He'd draw funny pictures of people for a couple of bucks apiece, often setting up his easel in the patio of the Taos Inn. And when business was slow there, he'd travel around the region doing the same thing—sometimes leaving my mom and me (and later my little sister Amy) for weeks at a time.

Those separations were hard on my mom, I know. And it was probably hard on me, too. But we managed. And when my dad came home—well, that was especially great. I'd sit in his studio while he painted and leafed through his old *MAD* magazines, looking at the pictures long before I could read. I'd draw or paint, too. And sometimes my dad would give me a lump of clay—not Play-Doh, but real clay. It was brown and hard at first. You really had to work with it before you could do much of anything with it. But with time and effort, it started to give in your hand, and you could roll it into snakes and squish it through your fingers and make all manner of beautiful and terrifying monsters with it. (As a bonus, the clay was extraordinarily messy.)

But my favorite memories? They took place when I was barely awake at all. This is what I remember:

My parents are in the front seat, driving home from a party. I stare out the window at the moon racing alongside, weaving through the trees. I watch as we gallop past familiar landmarks: the Baptist Church or the Piggly Wiggly . . . Doc Jones's deserted storefront . . . Mrs. Riggs's house. The car crunches down our dirt road and into our long driveway, past the concrete wall my dad built, past the weeping willows with their dripping branches. I close my eyes and pretend to sleep (or am I asleep?), and my dad gathers me up in his arms and carries me in, my eyelids slowly opening and closing as if they were buoys bobbing in gently swelling waves. He lays me in bed and my mom covers me up. Sometimes they whisper to each other, their words humming above my head.

I don't know if I've ever been as happy as in those moments. That defines my perfect peace. It defines, for me, a sense of *belonging*.

Depression often plants its seeds early. Sometimes, depression begets depression: Parents who suffer from it often pass it on to their children. (Scientists don't know whether it's genetic, or if a depressed parent unintentionally trains his or her children to be depressed, or both.) Sometimes, trauma lands like an asteroid into a child's life: She's forced to deal with an unimaginable loss or unspeakable abuse, and the child's mind and soul are forever scarred.

That wasn't me. Sure, I collected my share of hurts and fears, but I never doubted my parents' love for me. And if they were unreasonably stubborn about me eating my beans and beets? Well, I guess I could live with that.

But even so, I was a pretty weird kid.

I was born bookish. I think before I ever slept with my first stuffed animal, I was sleeping with books. I always needed eleven with me, for some reason—even in my crib. I made my mom count them out to make sure I wouldn't get shorted. I couldn't necessarily *read* them, of course, but it didn't matter. I loved the pictures. And remarkably, I only shredded one of them. I remember how satisfying it felt to tear apart my favorite book—the satisfying sound, the "*krrrrsh*" of Richard Scarry's drawings being torn into two parts, and threes, and fours. I hadn't realized that, once you tear something up, it's torn forever. Sometimes you can tape the pages, and my mom did so with some of them. But a few were gone forever. If you rip 'em out of the binding and turn them into confetti, it's nearly impossible to piece them back together again.

I guess the same could be said of people.

I had as much interest in sports as I had in tax audits. While other boys were learning how to hit baseballs and wrestling in the dirt, I was reading or drawing elaborate maps of strange, exotic, fantasy worlds. I had no idea that, for pure playground survival, I'd need to know how to catch a ball eventually.

All that introspective reading and imagining made me a pretty quiet child. For parents who liked their children to be "seen, not heard," I would've been example 1A. Of course, sometimes I wasn't seen, either. Once, when my Cub Scout leader was taking a passel of boys home from a den meeting, she forgot all about me. She dropped everyone else off and went back home. I'm glad she saw me as she shut the driver's side door. Otherwise, I might've spent the night in the back seat.

That would've been trouble, because I was a rather nervous child too. I was scared of mirrors, ghosts, water, and one of my dad's statues, which I was pretty sure wanted to eat me. I knew my parents would try to protect me, but with so many supernatural enemies just waiting to pounce, I knew they couldn't save me from every danger. No, I needed to take some responsibility for myself: I needed to be vigilant and crafty and, if the worst happened, steel myself for a tragic and untimely death. Childhood? A time of carefree innocence? Ha! I didn't even know how to tie my shoes, and yet I felt like I was just one stumble away from falling into a creepy H. P. Lovecraft yarn.

Just as it was so easy to lose myself in made-up worlds, I created terrors for this one. And that terrible talent of mine came into play when my family switched churches.

I enjoyed my family's first church a great deal. My parents were pretty active at Taos Presbyterian. My dad was an elder, my mom was forever shuffling bingo cards, and all my friends went to Sunday school with me. We sang "Jesus Loves Me" and heard gentle, affirming Bible stories and made Christmas decorations out of glitter.

Even the church service was more enjoyable than you'd think it'd be for a six-year-old. See, the minister quoted the apostle Paul a lot, but simply called him "Paul." The only Paul I knew was me, so I'd listen for the minister to drop my name and tell the congregation some bit of wisdom that, apparently, I'd come up with and had been passed on by dutiful congregants, a.k.a. my collection of admirers. I didn't remember saying most of these lovely, pious missives, but I was only six: I couldn't expect me to remember *everything* I said.

Yes, Taos Presbyterian did a fine job of instilling in me a sense of value and worth—perhaps, in some ways, too fine a job. I was quite convinced that I was very, *very* special. I knew that Jesus really did love me, because I was so worth loving. I belonged to Him.

Meanwhile, my dad was having a powerful religious epiphany of his own.

During one of his trips, he'd gone from being a Sunday-potluck sort of Christian to a Bible-beating, born-again, hold-up-your-hands-and-praise-the-Lord sort of Christian. This was great for him, of course, and eventually great for me, too. But even good change comes with its share of upheaval. While I cruised through my childhood in blissful ignorance, he was dumping wine down the sink, throwing away my comic books, and giving his last $20 to the poor. (My mom sternly reminded him—perhaps while she was packing her bags to leave him—that we were also poor, that he had a family to think about, and that the twenty bucks was supposed to buy gas for his next caricaturing gig.) And as I was listening for the minister to quote me, my father heard a whole bunch of things from our good reverend that I missed: that maybe heaven wasn't real, or that maybe Jesus didn't actually rise from the dead.

These were, naturally, serious theological issues—issues that definitely needed addressing. But when my dad started questioning the minister on his theology and challenging the church's direction, the elders kicked us out of church. We didn't belong anymore.

My mom lost many of her best friends during the drama, which was hard on her. I lost mine, too—though I didn't understand why. I just stopped going over to their houses, and they stopped coming to mine. I don't think this particularly traumatized me, but it did necessitate a recalibration. I made a couple of new friends that I didn't see quite as often, but mostly, I turned my attention inward. My imaginative life became more important. I grew more introverted.

Our new church impacted me the most, though.

In Taos, churchgoers had really only three bodies of worship to choose from: Catholic, Presbyterian, or Southern Baptist. We weren't going to convert to Catholicism, and the Presbyterians didn't want us. That left the Baptists, and inside its sanctuary was a whole different world.

The Presbyterian Church had been orderly and friendly—a place of firm handshakes and gentle chuckles. The Baptist Church felt like something between a Bosch painting and Costco on Saturday: loud, bustling, and just a half inch from falling into utter chaos. And if it was more theologically rigorous and still deeply loving, those Baptists showed a rougher, wilder sort of love than Taos's mild Presbyterians. Gone was "Jesus Loves Me" and old-timey fashion shows. This was an old-fashioned, God-fearing, fundamentalist church preparing for the end times. Anyone who was there just for the potlucks might as well go home and set up an Asherah pole, like King Manasseh did in 2 Chronicles 33.

A fire-and-brimstone pastor filled the pulpit—one who had little time for feel-good, do-nothing passages and gravitated toward stories about sin and judgment told in vivid, lurid detail. He had a particular fondness for Ahab and Jezebel, especially when the latter got thrown out a window and eaten by dogs. Stephen King could have taken lessons from our preacher.

As a seven-year-old (I'd learned, sorrowfully, that I was not the Paul quoted in church), I always favored exciting Old Testament stories to the kinder, gentler New Testament anyway. But in *this* Baptist church, Paul's letters took a back seat to bloody martyr-doms. And if the preacher ever taught on the Beatitudes, I've long since forgotten. The sermon I best remember (or think I remember, because the human mind is a strange and faulty thing) was all about what it meant to really pick up your cross and follow Jesus.

Jesus (so the preacher said) was hanging out with Peter, James, and John, and they climbed up this mountain. And on that mountain, the disciples saw something incredible—not the transfiguration that I've since read about, but a startling vision of the crucifixion (not Jesus', but theirs). They saw (according to the preacher, as translated or mistranslated in a seven-year-old's mind) themselves mirroring in their own lives, step for step, Christ's suffering and sacrifice. The whips. The nails. The hours upon hours of thirst and suffering.

And this wasn't necessarily Peter getting a fast-forward preview of his own martyrdom (he was crucified too, according to Christian tradition, only his crucifixion was very metal: upside-down). I got the distinct impression that this was what awaited them after they died. In order to get to heaven, they first needed to go through just about the worst hazing ceremony imaginable.

We could *all* look forward to that, I thought I heard. At least those of us who were going to the good place. Hate to think what awaited us in the bad place.

If we wanted to get into heaven, we had to show God just how much we wanted to be there. It wasn't enough to pick up our cross; we had to suffer and die on it, even though we had already died once. There was no other way.

Well.

Unless there's a passage of Scripture I've just been skipping over lo these many years, I likely misheard. But regardless of whether he *said* it or not, that's what I *heard*. And in the context of how it shaped me, that's what's important. For a little kid, this was a pretty startling revelation. It seemed cruel of God to ask that of a child (who knew, thanks to previous sermons and his own dark imagination, that he could kick the bucket at any time). But I knew that if God was anything, He was eminently fair, so there must be a reason, right? I wasn't old enough to really question the adults in my life—not my parents, not the teacher, not the preacher, and certainly not God himself. And even if I had doubts, I was a quiet child. I kept my own counsel.

I spent months thinking about this. After I went to bed and finished reading my eleven books, I contemplated this new existential terror in my life: not so much *why* this was, but *how*. How would it feel to be crucified? What was the worst part? Would it break the bones in my hands and feet, or just sort of shove them out of the way? My imagination became its own little theological horror movie. And I had other questions too. Would I have the courage to die like that when the time came? Would God give me courage? Would He help me through it? And most critically, if *this* is what I needed to go through to get through the pearly gates, did I even *want* to be a Christian?

But the alternative seemed pretty grim: Jezebel and the dogs and then, y'know, hell.

Eventually, I did decide to take the plunge—literally. I walked down the church aisle during one of its interminably long altar calls, all by myself. I felt the eyes of everyone as I practically sprinted down—terrified of the attention, terrified of my future. I was seven years old.

I used to tell people that I took that walk because I wanted to see what the baptismal (hidden behind the altar) looked like from the other side. And that's at least partly true. I think I also liked, in some ways, the idea of all the attention I'd get. Anyone who ever went down the aisle would get a nice round of applause afterward. I missed my days being quoted from the pulpit.

But as I walked quickly down the aisle, I also knew what I was doing—the horrible, terrifying commitment I was making. I wasn't just walking down the aisle: I was walking toward eventual death and crucifixion and, finally, heaven. At an age when I didn't know what separation meant, I still knew that to be separated from God for all eternity was an awful thing. I was willing to do anything to preserve that connection. To feel like I belonged to Him. And when the pastor knelt down beside me to talk to me—with all the congregation listening in, with my mom and dad somewhere in the sea of people, invisible and separate—I couldn't say a word. I was crying too hard.

When you struggle with depression, faith can be of tremendous help. To know that you're loved and cherished by the Creator of all things—to have confidence that you were made for a purpose in God's divine plan—can keep us going when our static-filled mind tells us to stop.

But sometimes, even honest faith can be twisted into something God never wanted or meant for it to be.

It's said that most people draw their idea of who God is from their fathers. I wrote a book with someone who grew up with a distant, hard-to-please dad. When he first started exploring the concept of Christianity, he was asked about the first thing he thought of when he thought of God.

"I see Him frowning at me," the man said.

I was so fortunate to have the father I had—one so full of laughter and care and love. He made me feel precious. When I pictured—and picture—God, I picture my heavenly Father not just smiling, but *laughing*, just like my earthly one so often does. I think that his example gave me the psychological backbone to deal with the strangeness and pain that religion often brings with it. He gave me the ability to see a loving God behind the legalism and hypocrisy and inconsistency that we, as fallen, fallible humans, often bring to faith.

But at the edges of my being, at maybe too early an age, I began to understand how serious sin was, too, and what a rupture it can cause between us and the Almighty. From (mis)hearing my Baptist pastor, I learned all about judgment before I learned about grace, and internalized that even God's grace comes with a heavy hand. I felt the weight of responsibility to be a good person, even though we'd also been taught that there's no way we can be good enough.

Jesus loved me, this I knew. But I was a broken thing. And as a child with his share of mangled toys, I knew that *my* broken things, even if I bothered to keep them, would never be loved in quite the same way. I was grateful that I was loved anyway, in spite of that brokenness. But honestly, that love felt a lot more like pity.

According to the hypersexual theories of Sigmund Freud, not much happens between your sixth and eleventh birthdays. Those years are part of a stage he called latency. "Things cool down, so to speak," wrote Adam Cash.[3]

That, of course, is a load of bunk. Sure, not much of Freud's sexualized theories are in play then. But the American Psychological Association suggests that kids between the ages of six and ten are exploring their environments, along with getting more closely acquainted with themselves. They're beginning to appreciate the importance of the wide world around them and are trying to figure out where they fit in that world. Their relationships outside home and family take on much greater importance, and their own self-concept grows beyond what Mom and Dad think. They, according to the APA's website "are able to view themselves based on: how they perform in school; capacity to make friends; and their physical appearance."[4]

When I was seven, those three criteria—school, friends, looks—were in pretty good shape. By the time I turned nine, they were in shambles.

The looks were the first to go.

When I was six or seven I was, quite simply, an adorable child—the Ryan Reynolds of the primary school set. You think *your* kid is cute? Bah.

But then my front teeth started sticking out, and some children started calling me Bugs Bunny.

But I wasn't too put out. Sure, maybe I wasn't *cute* anymore, but it's not like I was dating at the time. I was doing well in school. I had my friends. And my self-mandated crucifixion was still, hopefully, well down the road.

And then we moved.

After Taos, Colorado Springs felt like the Big City, full of paved roads and stoplights, buildings with more than one story and—the pinnacle of space-age technology—escalators. I could've spent days riding up and down those suckers. In terms of the cosmopolitan wow factor, Colorado Springs felt like a major step up.

But if the Springs felt like Paris, Bristol Elementary felt like Pluto.

In Taos, I had been used to sitting in one classroom with one primary teacher. That's pretty typical, I think. But Bristol was on the Colorado Springs vanguard of exploring new educational techniques: Instead of individual classrooms, third graders were thrown into what was called an "open classroom," where teaching areas were divided by tables and low bookcases, if they were defined at all. We were still all lumped into groups, I think, but we rotated through this open space while the teachers stayed put. One group might start the day with science in one spot, for instance. Then when science was done, we'd pick up our stuff and tromp over to the math area.

The concept was all about fostering creativity and allowing for more one-on-one attention between teachers and the students who needed it most.[5] If I had started the year there, maybe it would've worked. But I was already plenty creative, and instead of being given one-on-one attention, I didn't get any. I was a latecomer, and I got lost in the system—a kid who fell off the educational train between teaching areas. If everyone stood up and rumbled to another area, I'd often get up and rumble too—but there was no guarantee I'd rumble to the right place. I'd get lost on the way to math and wind up in art class, carving whales out of soap. And sometimes, I'd just stay in the same spot. Since no one seemed to care where I went, and since I didn't particularly care for where I should go, it seemed like a win-win to just stay put and read.

And naturally, I started to struggle, especially in math. I went from feeling like one of the smartest kids in Taos to one of the dumbest in Bristol.

Most of the other third graders had no idea what to do with this weird, quiet, bucktoothed kid who'd wander dreamily around the school. I broke all rules of conformity, and let's face it: No social group prizes conformity as much as preteens do. I was different, weird, something *other*, the third-grade equivalent of a leper.

He is unclean. He shall live alone.

But I couldn't always be alone.

The bus ride to and from school was almost always a low point. I had to sit beside someone who, more than likely, didn't want to sit by me. And if he had friends around, I felt a little like a duck that had waddled into the water—smack-dab next to a school of piranhas.

One afternoon, four or five guys thought it'd be funny to pretend to spit in my hair. And oh, how they laughed when one actually did. I sat as small and still as I could, trying to smile, trying to pretend like we were all in on a fun joke. That I was included, for a little while, in their group.

But the hurt and shame burbled up in me, like the stuff we put in one of those papier-mâché volcanoes we'd make in science class.

Funny how, when it comes to how we feel about ourselves, we sometimes ignore the people who know us the best and instead trust strangers on the bus.

Most adults think that bullying is just a normal part of growing up, and in a way, they're right: It's certainly common to be bullied. The rates vary wildly from study to study, but according to a 2016 report by the National Center for Educational Statistics, about one in every five kids experiences some sort of bullying.[6] Being a bookish and—let's face it—scrawny kid, I probably attracted more than my fair share of unwanted attention. But what I experienced as a child—before, during, and after Bristol—was not that rare and not that severe compared to some. No one ever beat me up. No one ever stole my lunch money.

But in Bristol, I didn't have any real backstop until I got home. And bullying—common or not, normal or not—can have a huge impact well into adulthood on those bullied.

According to a 2014 study out of Duke and Warwick Universities, kids who were bullied had far higher levels of depression and anxiety disorders into young adulthood than kids who weren't.[7] Nearly 25 percent of those who were bullied reported having suicidal thoughts as adults, compared to less than 6 percent of those who'd never been bullied, according to the study. (Incidentally, other studies show that lots of bullied kids become bullies themselves, and they also suffer higher rates of depression and anxiety.[8])

And the problem is only getting worse.

Once I got off that bus, I was safe. Even that day, I probably snuck up to the bathroom to wash my hair out, poured myself a bowl of cereal and watched cartoons for a while, the shame draining out of me slowly. We probably ate dinner as a family, because we almost always did, and I was able to feel a part of something again. I might've played a game with my little sister, because *she*, at least, still thought I was pretty cool. As wild as the seas at school got, I knew I had a harbor to sail to.

Today, most kids don't necessarily have that harbor—not like they used to, anyway. Fewer families eat together, and thanks to social media, children can be bullied twenty-four hours a day. We live in an age when most youth with access to a smartphone will check them first thing in the morning, and it'll be the last thing they look at before they go to sleep. Many teens even sleep *with* them—waking up and answering whenever they hear the telltale chime of a message.[9] This dependency on technology isn't healthy, of course: Experts say that teens are sleeping less because of it. But as kids spend less time physically interacting with their friends, phones form a tether to their lives.

If their lives turn ugly, though, those same phones can become a conduit for bullying—a pipeline that's open 24/7. While most of us would see an obvious solution to that problem—*turn off the phone*—for youth it's not so easy. Because so much social interaction takes place online, losing the phone can be just as isolating as the bullying is, or worse. And while most studies show that cyberbullying is a little less frequent than traditional bullying (bullies still apparently value that personal touch), those who are cyberbullied are likely to be bullied in person, too.[10]

Is it any wonder that rates of depression among children and teens are on the rise?[11]

I had another advantage a lot of kids today don't, as well: a stay-at-home mom who was keeping a close eye on me.

I wasn't about to unload all my grievances to my parents. To me, it would have been an admission of failure. But even if I didn't tell my parents much, my mom wasn't dumb. And when I brought home my first—and last—report card from Bristol, she knew something was wrong. She went to school with me a couple of days later and observed me and my class in action.

It must have been pretty boring, because I didn't actually do anything all day. Not. A. Thing. While the rest of the kids were shouting and talking and asking questions and shouting some more (there was a lot of shouting, Mom tells me), I just sat, reading a book—ignored by teacher and student alike. I was divorced, it seems, from the entire school.

"After spending that morning in your classroom," she said, "I immediately decided we were going to get you out of that school, no matter what."

But in some respects, the work was done. The seeds had been sown. I wasn't depressed then. But Bristol and that terrifying sermon had reshaped part of my character. The way I looked at the world, and the way I looked at myself, had been fundamentally changed. I knew that God loved me, but for some reason He wanted me to suffer. I knew that I was different from the other kids, and being different was bad. I grew anxious not just of ghosts and statues, but people, too. I believed they wouldn't like me. I knew they didn't want me around. And even if they said they did, they couldn't be trusted. They might just want to make fun of me. It might be a trap.

I review movies for a living, and I've seen my share of cinematic exorcisms. "Possession" has long been a horror-movie staple. And sometimes, depression can feel that way: Something outside of you—something other—invades who you are and takes you over.

But I think that obscures a more critical truth. In fact, *all* of us are possessed, in a way: We are in possession of our own selves. Each day, our experiences mold us and shape us into who we are and, perhaps, who we can be. We bear the joys and responsibilities and burdens of what we've made of ourselves—and how others have molded us too. We are products of many hands. Some of those hands help give us the strength and virtue we need. They help mold us into something closer to the people we want to be, and the people that God always designed us to be. Others twist us or bend us out of shape, sometimes where we feel like we're beyond recognition. And sometimes the work they do never really gets kneaded out.

And sometimes, the people who make us better and the people who make us worse . . . sometimes they're the very same.

That was my misshapen self I was working with in third grade—a kid who'd just been saddled with a big dollop of ugliness and self-doubt. That's the clay I had to work with. And naturally, as I tried to cover up all that ugliness or reshape it somehow, that further twisted the final work.

I wasn't depressed then. Just sad and scared sometimes. But as I grew, that sadness and fear grew into something else. And the first hints of it were right around the corner.

CHAPTER 4

OF BRAIN AND BLOOD

The Bluebird of Happiness long absent from his life,
Ned is visited by the Chicken of Depression.

GARY LARSON, *The Far Side*

LET'S BE HONEST: Depression, as miserable and as debilitating as it can be, is also pretty boring.

Imagine being a famous Hollywood director—particularly an explosion-loving one like Michael Bay—tasked with turning a realistic depiction of depression into the next summer blockbuster and you're given this scene:

The dorm room is dark. The door is shut, the curtains are drawn. Only a digital alarm clock glows in the corner. It reads 3:37 a.m. Lying on the top bunk is a young man staring at the ceiling. That's it. Just staring. He's not slept for twenty-four hours. He's not eaten for thirty-two. He hasn't showered in three days.

The camera pans to the clock again. It reads 7:14 a.m.
The camera zooms in on the man, staring at the ceiling.
Back to the clock, which now reads 9:25 a.m., and . . .

Clearly, this is a scene in need of some ninjas.

My freshman year of college, I was the star of that particularly scintillating scene. If a pack of ninjas knocked on my door that morning, I'd ignore all their shouted Japanese curses, just like I ignored most knocks on my door. If the masked assassins somehow jimmied the door open with one of their sharp little stars, leapt in, and started brandishing their samurai swords, I'd simply turn over and stare at the wall for a bit, praying they'd either go away and leave me alone or run me through and be done with it.

Ninjas, as hard as it is to fathom, had lost their charm for me. Nearly everything had.

But funny thing: I didn't think I was depressed. I only thought I was in love.

But be it love or depression, it's best to back up a bit.

When we last left me, I was escaping Bristol Elementary and moving into a new school better suited to me (or so my parents hoped): Whittier Elementary.

It was certainly an improvement over my old school; I could see that right away. No one was spitting in my hair, and I could walk home all by myself; no need to ride a bus. But for the first month, I didn't talk to anyone unless someone made me. For weeks, I spent recess sitting by myself under a tree, throwing pea gravel at my shoes.*

---

* I pretended my feet were spaceships, and the pea gravel were photon torpedos.

I wasn't depressed. And I wasn't seeing a therapist. But looking back, I'd wager I was wildly and clinically anxious.

If I'm right, I certainly wouldn't be alone. About 6.4 percent of American kids between the ages of six and seventeen were diagnosed with anxiety in 2011,[1] a rate that is increasing over time. And experts believe that anxiety, like depression, often goes undiagnosed. Experts also say that depression and anxiety are often linked. Like those creepy twins in *The Shining*, they walk hand in hand together, inviting those nearby to play. Anxiety is a symptom of chronic depression.[2] But depression is sometimes brought on by anxiety too. About 50 percent of folks diagnosed with depression also suffer from some sort of anxiety disorder, according to the Anxiety and Depression Association of America.[3]

My anxiety du jour at the time was probably something akin to (and still is, to some extent) social anxiety disorder. Simply put, it's the desire to bring a security blanket to every party, curl up in a corner, and hide under it until everyone goes home. It's a few steps beyond regular ol' shyness or introversion: It moves from being uncomfortable to being incapable. I've been unable to attend dinners and get-togethers and, one time in college, nearly ran away from a surprise party thrown in my honor. (Awkward, I know.) In sixth grade, I finished a series of classes to join our family church. But when we arrived at the church for the ceremony, I got so sick that I couldn't go through with it. I spent the evening in the bathroom as my worried parents wondered whether I'd had a change of heart and decided to become a Taoist instead.

I'm able to get through most social situations these days, and sometimes even enjoy them, but I still spend weeks dreading them—even the parties my wife and I throw. In social situations, I often feel like my mouth and body are being operated by a bevy of blind, drunken gnomes. I've worked up a variety of standard small-talk answers to standard small-talk questions, but if you ask me something off-script, I just might utter a series of completely disconnected syllables or suddenly dash off to the bathroom to hide. And even if it is a pretty standard question—"How are you?" for instance—I might forget or ignore the right response ("Just great. And how are you?") and say something off book. Any book. "Muhuhduhoo," for instance. Or "Grust jate. And cow were me?" Or "I'm writing a book about depression. Do you want to hear about the flaws of the open classroom system?"

I spend more time plotting out party strategy than Patton did his invasion of Italy.

Luckily, most normal people like talking about themselves. So if you really hate talking at parties, just get good at asking questions. If you press the right buttons you might not need to talk again for the rest of the evening.

But before I hit puberty, I had no script. I didn't even know I could make up a script. Unless I was really on my game, or really comfortable with the folks I was with, "Muhuhduhoo" was pretty much my standard response to most questions. Or, at least, I feared it would be. Other new kids could lean on sports for social access, but I was lousy at those. In gym, I was always stuck in the outfield with twenty other uncoordinated kids, and if a ball managed to find its way toward me, I'd suddenly contort like a smashed spider, arms and legs all curled up, while the ball thunked softly at my feet. I was getting uglier by the hour too. By the time I hit fourth grade, I was pretty sure that my relatively normal childhood in Taos was an anomaly and that an abnormal child like me wasn't going to get anywhere in elementary social circles. I wasn't just the new kid: I was the weird kid, and I felt like I was getting weirder by the day.

But before I had worn out my shoes by throwing gravel at

them, a couple of fellow fourth graders—Chris and Bret—came and took pity on me. They asked if I wanted to play with them, and so I did.

I found a backstop that kept my psyche from rolling right down the street. I might've been weird, but I had a couple of weird people to hang out with. And that made a huge difference. It might not sound like much to you. But to me, it was nothing short of a miracle.

That began a period of slow, mostly steady recovery.

I made it through elementary school and landed in junior high, where most everyone's a little dysfunctional. I might have started experiencing the first signs of depression: falling grades, unexplained sicknesses, irritability, and spending lots of time in my room. But depression can be difficult to differentiate from regular adolescence.[4] Was I tired all the time because I was depressed? Or was I tired because I was growing like a weed and I needed more sleep? Did I spend a lot of time in my room because I was depressed, or was it because I liked to be alone and enjoyed reading and (at age thirteen) my parents had gotten lamer and my sister was annoying? Not every bad mood is depression. Not every bit of momentary neurosis needs a name.

And even if my depression had dug in its first roots, it seemed to get better as I grew. By the time I was in high school, I felt like I was one of the more sane, happy kids I knew.

But while I might not have been particularly depressed as a teen, plenty of youth are. The emotional highs and lows and physical changes that come with adolescence, the heightened importance of peers, and the friction kids often have with parents all conspire to make the teen years really difficult for many. About 20 percent of teens suffer from depression at some point growing up,[5] with females suffering from it twice as often as males. And as we talked about before, depressed teens often become troubled adults.

But first they have to *make* it to adulthood.

Suicide rates among teens are breaking all the wrong sorts of records: Never, according to the *Los Angeles Times*, have teenagers been killing themselves in such numbers—or at least not since 1960, when the government started tracking it.[6] According to The Jason Foundation's Parent Research Program, suicide is now the second leading cause of death among youth between the ages of ten and twenty-four.[7] In 2019, the Ohio Department of Health reported that suicide was the leading cause of death among kids ages ten to fourteen in the state.[8] I've read stories of kids as young as nine killing themselves.[9]

Is your listless middle schooler depressed? Is your cranky teen despairing? Not necessarily. But concerned parents should do three things, I think.

First, watch for the warning signs. Anger and irritability; social withdrawal; increased sensitivity to rejection or criticism; fatigue; unexplained physical ailments such as headaches or stomachaches; changes in appetite; a retreat from extracurricular activities (or, sometimes, a sudden and alarming increase in them).

Second, talk with your teen. Easier said than done, right? But if you can manage it, good communication is key. If your son or daughter feels comfortable talking with you during the middle-school and high-school years, you'll be able to keep tabs on his or her state of mind. And if your teen expresses feelings of worthlessness or hopelessness, talks about having trouble sleeping or having a hard time concentrating, or confesses to having thoughts of hurting himself or herself, those are critical signs that your child might be depressed. Additionally, just those lines of communication can actually help *stave off* depression a bit. They can help your child feel less alone, less isolated. Your teen can express some of the angst and despair she or he might feel, and it's almost always healthy to let that stuff breathe.

So ask lots of questions—about school, friends, and your teen's state of mind. It doesn't hurt to ask even really awkward questions: "Have you ever thought about hurting yourself?" A friend of mine, who used to lead a suicide prevention nonprofit for teens, says that these sorts of questions can open the door to really important, critical conversations. You're the parent: It's your job to be a little nosy.

Keep in mind, though, that even when your kids love you and value your opinion and might secretly long for some help or even just a hug from you, they still might not talk about these deeply personal, painful issues. (I know I didn't.) Just as parents sometimes try to protect their children from life's ooky realities, so children and teens sometimes try to protect their parents. Sometimes, they don't want you to worry about them . . . even if you should. But keep at it. Ask lots of questions. Reveal little bits about yourself—the stuff that scares you or makes you sad (up to a point). If you show that you trust your kids enough to reveal the chinks in your own armor, your kids will be a little more likely to show you that same trust. And finally, be available to talk as much as possible. Take walks. Encourage conversation on the way to school. Eat meals together without the TV on. Be there.

Third, when in doubt, see a professional. Take your child to a counselor or psychologist. Be proactive, even if it's a little awkward. A mental health expert can give you far more tools to help your son or daughter through those really trying adolescent years. If your child needs help, get that help. And honestly, I'd always err on the safe side.

Another thing to mention here: Depression and drug or alcohol abuse often go hand in hand. According to the National Institute on Drug Abuse, alcohol and drug addicts are twice as likely to be depressed, and depressed people are twice as likely to suffer from addiction.[10] While the relationship between mental health and addiction (like everything surrounding depression, it seems) can be pretty multilayered, it seems as though it can be a little bit of a chicken-and-egg thing. People with addiction issues can feel worthless and depressed because of their addictions. But folks suffering from depression—particularly in their teen years, according to many experts—can turn to alcohol and drugs as a method of self-medication.[11] When you get drunk or abuse drugs, those feelings of worthlessness can ebb away for a time . . . even though they will later lead to feelings of worthlessness (or circumstances that trigger that sense of worthlessness), which drives people to drink or get high again.

Antoine de Saint-Exupéry summed up this vicious cycle as well as anyone in his classic children's book *The Little Prince*:

> *"Why are you drinking?" demanded the little prince.*
> *"So that I may forget," replied the tippler.*
> *"Forget what?" inquired the little prince, who was already sorry*
> *   for him.*
> *"Forget that I am ashamed," the tippler confessed, hanging his*
> *   head.*
> *"Ashamed of what?" insisted the little prince, who wanted to*
> *   help him.*
> *"Ashamed of drinking!"*[12]

We don't know when the tippler began drinking, of course: The Little Prince isn't privy to his backstory. But I'd bet that, like most addictions and many mental illnesses, it is rooted in the tippler's teen years.

I was fortunate to escape that corrosive outlet in high school and college. None of my friends in high school drank or used drugs, and they would've been mad at me if I had. And while some of my friends did drink and smoke weed in college, I never saw either as a worthwhile or desirable escape. The one time I got truly drunk—as a freshman, through beer and banana-flavored schnapps, I believe—I was so sick that night that I never had the urge to over-imbibe again. Another neurosis of mine proved to be actually helpful: I'm kinda phobic about throwing up. For me, hanging my head in sadness was always preferable to hanging it over a toilet.

My family and friends carried me through junior high and high school well. By my senior year, I felt like I'd locked most of my early insecurities in a tiny psychic closet. I wasn't quite as ugly and awkward as I'd been. I wrote funny columns for the school paper that people seemed to like—giving me the sense that I knew how to do something pretty well, at least. And writing fit my personality: Few skills value introversion as much as writing. Sure, if I became a sportswriter or something, I'd probably have to talk with people occasionally, but it felt like a navigable career choice. I figured I'd go into journalism, win a few Pulitzers, and move on at age thirty-five to become a beloved and extravagantly rich novelist.

But first, I figured I had to go to college.

Hastings College—a tiny liberal arts school in the eastern part of Nebraska—seemed perfect. It was far enough from Colorado Springs to feel like I was really on my own, but close enough that, if I really needed to come home, I could. It was smaller than my high school, which felt comforting. I guessed it didn't have the drinking or drug culture that a big public school would have. And its name—Hastings—felt vaguely upper-crust and prestigious, like an Ivy League also-ran. Hastings? Harvard? They sounded a little alike, right?

Most importantly, none of my good friends would be going there. I could figure out who I was away from my phalanx of emotional backstops. I would learn if I could survive and succeed on my own.

And here's the big surprise: It worked! I did make new friends. I loved most of my classes and found new interests that I never imagined.

But none of that stopped depression from barging into my life. It was no longer the creepy little twins from *The Shining* asking for me to come play. It was a full-blown monster, smoking in my bed and playing punk music at 3 a.m. I could not ignore it or push it away. It was there.

Four months after I arrived, I was lying in that dark dorm room, listening to friends hammer on the door and wishing they, everyone, everything, would just go away.

In *The Noonday Demon*, Andrew Solomon writes, "I did not experience depression until I had pretty much solved my problems."[13] That felt like me, too. I had no reason to be unhappy. I wasn't plagued by the insecurities of my childhood. No one had died. My life felt on track.

But the move, and the radical changes it brought, triggered something inside me. I wasn't lonely, but I felt alone. I was doing well in my classes but felt kinda worthless anyway. My whole life was in front of me, and all I could see was years and years worth of monotonous work. I was an adult now, and I didn't much like the look of it.

I also had the misfortune of falling in love.

Her name was Wendy, and she was obviously the wrong woman for me. I could see that immediately. I listened to '60s folk music; she absorbed a steady stream of pop. I imagined myself dreamy and deep and somewhat artistically tortured; her favorite color was pink and she smiled all the time. I was a literature major with minors in history and philosophy; she was all about chemistry and math.

She also had a boyfriend. No matter—not for the confident and heelish guy I was. I asked her out anyway. She announced that she was very happy with her significant other, thanks. And that was that.

But it wasn't. Not for me. I tried to forget her and move on—I went to a college with loads of far more suitable girlfriends—but I couldn't. My melancholia twined with my infatuation until they became one and the same. I fell into a deep and unhealthy state of longing that felt like a literal form of lovesickness. Perhaps it didn't help that so many of my favorite writers back then—the true Romantic-era writers such as Byron and Shelley and Keats—treated love and despair like some fatal curse; perhaps it didn't help that so many of them died so young. Even today, I wonder how much of my state of mind then was love, how much was the curious, natural workings of my mind, and how much was that blasted Alfred Tennyson.

But it didn't matter, since the whole stew led me to the same place: a full-blown depressive episode. I couldn't eat; I couldn't sleep. Every waking minute was filled with thoughts of her. No, not of her, but how empty my life was without her. And that's a very different thing. A very selfish thing.

And that's when I spent most of my days in that dark room, staring at the ceiling and waiting for ninjas. I felt like I was dying. At eighteen, my life was over unless I could finally get some resolution.

So, in the midst of my depression, in what I considered a pretty gutsy move, I laid it all out on the line for her. I sat with her on a back staircase of her dorm and told her that I loved her. I needed her. I didn't see how I could live without her—but I had to figure out a way to try if the answer was absolutely, positively no.

She told me she needed time to think. The next night, she announced she was coming by my dorm room to give me her decision. I quickly showered, sprayed some air freshener around the room, and waited until I heard her knock. I welcomed her in and we sat on my floor.

And the answer was absolutely, positively no.

"No," she said. "I'm so sorry. I'm with someone else. I want to honor that."

I thought about it for a minute, trying to decide whether I should cry now or later.

And then I chose a third option: I leaned over and kissed her—planted one right on her lips, just like I always saw in the movies.

We've been together almost every day since.

That's the story I tell, and it's true. But there's another story lurking underneath.

Yes, Wendy and I were together. But my depression didn't leave. It was the proverbial third wheel in our relationship—the thing that would exacerbate every disagreement and play on every insecurity, on every bit of shame and guilt I felt. I had thought that I was miserable because I couldn't be with the girl I loved, but that wasn't true. Love, even requited love, isn't enough to wipe away a brain filled with shame and insecurity. It can mask it for a time, but depression often comes unmoored from circumstance. Events can trigger it, but it often lingers far longer. So even when I was with that girl, that culmination of my romantic quest, my weird little brain didn't say, "Well, now, all is right with the world." It just found new things to obsess about.

Before Wendy and I started going out, when I was languishing in my dorm room, I told myself that Wendy was unreachable, untouchable for the likes of someone like me. I didn't deserve her. Maybe I wasn't *completely* unlovable. But I couldn't be loved by somebody like her.

So when she did kinda sorta seem to like me, it totally freaked me out. Clearly, she was as messed up as I was. Either that or I had fooled her into thinking I was an okay sort of chap. And it was only a matter of time before she figured it out.

Soon, the time I spent with her was filled with anxiety and jealousy. I worried she still had feelings for her ex. I fretted she might fall in love with someone else. I grew jealous of her time: I knew that every minute she spent with someone who wasn't me would be a chance for her to realize her horrific mistake, to realize that someone—heck, anyone—was a better fit for her than I was. And I'd be worse off than before. As I grew more needy and self-pitying, I could well have driven her away. I probably should have.

Also, we started having sex.

I had slowly drifted away from God in college, as lots of us do.[14] I wasn't going to church and was questioning a lot of what I had been taught. But those lessons hold on tightly. My parents had raised me to believe sex was reserved for marriage. And so when Wendy and I started sleeping together, the dissonance between the person I felt that I *should be* and the person I *was* reached a critical level. Deep down, even in my more agnostic state, I knew I was disappointing God. And just as importantly, I was betraying my parents. If they found out, I knew how ashamed they'd be. I wasn't being the man they'd raised me to be. And the weight of that reality was crushing.

"I don't really understand myself," Paul says in Romans 7:15, "for I want to do what is right, but I don't do it. Instead, I do what I hate" (NLT).

I didn't hate sex. I really, *really* liked it. But I hated that I liked it, and I hated that I was doing it. The sin hung around my being like one of those old-fashioned ball and chains that prisoners used to wear. Mornings after were filled with guilt and shame. *I'm not going to do that anymore*, I'd tell myself. *Never again.*

And then we'd do it again.

Depression magnifies your shame and insecurities and tells you that you're fatally flawed, inherently unlovable. And as the disease closes its bony fingers around your brain, those lies slowly squeeze into a semblance of truth. She could see I wasn't doing well—that I was sometimes ridiculously jealous, sometimes kinda cruel, sometimes mysteriously withdrawn. But she didn't know the depths of it.

When I started cutting, she never even saw.

I blame *The Abyss* for my turn to the knife.

James Cameron's best film (sorry, *Titanic* fans) takes us underwater and on a search for strange, intelligent, and possibly dangerous creatures who live in its deepest recesses. But as often happens in these sorts of movies, the real monster is us. In this case, it was Lt. Coffey (played by Michael Biehn), a Navy SEAL commander whose sanity is slowly unraveling under pressure—literally, the pressure of the deep blue sea, which can cause psychosis.

In one scene, he sits at a table. He stares with intense concentration at someone who's speaking, his face slightly contorted in what we first assume is anger. But then the camera pans toward the floor, and we see what Coffey's doing under the table: drawing a massive knife across his forearm, leaving long stripes of blood.

Why would someone do that? a normal moviegoer might ask. And certainly, Cameron meant to show the guy's slow, inevitable descent into insanity.

But as I watched, I drew a different conclusion: *He's trying to drain the crazy away.*

I didn't feel *crazy*, but I knew I wasn't *right*. When I looked at my life reasonably and rationally, I knew I had very few problems: I was in a serious relationship with a great girl. My grades were good, my profs tolerated me, and my friends seemed to like me. I was watching *The Abyss* with a bunch of them.

But I felt that weird something inside me, swirling like a black poison. I felt the noise of depression grow in my temples, pressing against my eyes like a balloon blown too big.

In earlier days, doctors would use leeches on their patients—draining them of their more toxic humours to restore balance. Ancient monks used to practice self-flagellation—whipping or scourging themselves as a form of punishment and purification, to scour away their stubborn sins and worthlessness.

Sure, I knew that leeches and self-mortification weren't exactly in style these days. But the idea of that visceral pain—to feel something that might drown out the rising static in my brain—was attractive. It even felt urgent. For my good, and for everyone else's, I needed to drain the crazy away.

In this, like so many other aspects of my life, I was a late bloomer. Cutting often begins in the teens, and experts say it's happening earlier and earlier. As was the case for me, outside influences—be they the entertainment we see or the friends we keep—can lead youth to experiment.[15] Few kids are watching *The Abyss* these days, but cutting has gone mainstream. And while many would say it's an important issue that should be discussed, that very discussion can both introduce it and normalize it to teens who'd never otherwise engage.

And some experts say it's getting more popular. Karen Conterio, coauthor of the book *Bodily Harm*, says she can go into any school in the country and ask a random teen if he or she knows anyone who cuts. "Yeah, everybody knows someone," Conterio says.[16] It, like depression, is more common among girls. But guys can be prone to it too. It can be connected to bipolar and eating disorders, compulsive tendencies, and, quite naturally, depression.[17] Cutting is an extreme response to high-level stress or unmanageable emotion, and often it's done by people who feel, as I did, unable or unwilling to talk about what's going on in their lives. They don't feel like they have the ability or the vocabulary to deal with the pain inside. So they scrape a more manageable, more understandable pain on their arm or leg or stomach.

Bodily Harm's other coauthor, Wendy Lader, unpacked the profile of a cutter for WebMD: "They may have a history of sexual, physical, or verbal abuse," she said. "Many are sensitive, perfectionists, overachievers. The self-injury begins as a defense against what's going on in their family, in their lives. They have failed in one area of their lives, so this is a way to get control."[18]

Control. Experts use that term a lot when it comes to cutting.

The act seems baffling to those on the outside: *Why would kids want to hurt themselves?* parents ask. And I totally get that reaction.

But I remember the first time I picked up that knife too—a kitchen knife, a blade just like the one I sold door-to-door for a few weeks to earn money for college. I don't remember if there was a specific trigger or not, but I do remember hurting, feeling like my life and perhaps even my brain was spinning out of my control. I felt like failure was an inescapable part of who I was, and the sense of stress and shame that went along with that failure was building up inside like pus in a pimple. I needed to pop it.

I knew my parents would be ashamed of what I was doing. My old friends were all hundreds of miles away, and my new ones thought I was pretty normal. I couldn't even let Wendy know: I was sure, if she knew how screwed up I was, she'd drop me and run screaming, back to her old, surely more sane, boyfriend. In the moment, cutting felt like my only recourse—the only thing I could do to re-establish an element of control.

But—and this is funny if you think about it—I really hate pain.

As such, I was never a particularly spectacular or convincing cutter. My cutting never amounted to more than a handful of shallow, red, barely bleeding scratches—not much worse than a particularly angry cat might inflict. And the process always left me feeling rather disappointed. From a purely aesthetic point of view, my ill-planned hatchmarks didn't look nearly as cool as Lt. Coffey's bright-red stripes. Sometimes I did feel better, the same way that smashing your thumb with a hammer will make a headache disappear. Kids who cut often report a sense of relief after cutting— a feeling that some of that emotional angst drains away—and I think I did feel that, too. Otherwise, I never would have returned to the practice, and I did. For a couple of years in college—when my brain felt like it was boiling over—cutting was the only way I knew to turn down the heat.

But the act left me confused and ashamed, too, another sign that I wasn't quite right. I never felt measurably less crazy. In fact, the cuts on my arm reminded me all the time that I was far from sane.

And yet, deep inside, a part of me told me that, maybe, I just wasn't doing it right. It chided me for my lack of courage. *Maybe*, I thought to myself, *if I just cut deeper* . . .

It never occurred to me to, y'know, *see* somebody about these issues. Only about a third of people dealing with severe depression ever do.[19] We feel alone, and so we suffer alone.

And yet, I eventually felt better.

Oh, my depression wasn't cured. I would've needed help from some actual mental health experts to facilitate that, I think. And by college, it had settled down in my brain for a nice, long stay. But it did find a nice spare mental room and kept its door mostly closed: It wasn't playing the accordion in my psychic living space anymore.

Three critical elements in my life, I think, helped me come out of it.

One might have simply been the passage of time.

Big depressive episodes can be a little like our own personal earthquakes. They rock your world. But sometimes—at least in my case—the most acute manifestations of depression can ease if you just hold on and push through for long enough. The weeks I spent in my dark dorm room staring at the ceiling was college's San Andreas Fault–like "big one." The rest of college was filled with the after-shocks. But as time went on, they grew less severe, less traumatic.

The second—likely interrelated—was Wendy.

She didn't know how insecure I was. But as our relationship stretched into weeks, then months, then years, my anxieties about losing her began to subside. I wasn't good enough for her. But for Wendy, that didn't seem to matter. She had thrown her lot in with me, and by golly, she was going to stick with me no matter what.

"Love is a decision, it is a judgment, it is a promise," author Erich Fromm wrote in *The Art of Loving*. "If love were only a feeling, there would be no basis for the promise to love each other forever. A feeling comes and it may go. How can I judge that it will stay forever, when my act does not involve judgment and decision."[20]

Before I met Wendy, I had always thought that love was an emotion—something that you accepted with passivity and gave without effort. You love someone because you do. You love someone because he or she's inherently lovable. And if you really love someone, it's because (I thought) you're meant for each other—like two puzzle pieces cut from the same picture. Even the phrase *soul mate*—a term I very much used back then—conveys this sense of divine purpose and fate. Love, if it's real, is an inevitability.

I don't think that anymore.

Wendy and I weren't soul mates. Look at who we were, and we went together about as well as peanut butter and mayonnaise. Moreover, I was hardly lovable. I seemed to make myself more unlovable the more we saw each other—almost as if I was testing her resolve.

But she loved me anyway. Maybe that kiss started that love in motion. But it was her decision—one imbued with strength and sacrifice—that was the real love in our relationship.

For me, our relationship was a case of love at first sight. For her, it was a decision she made every day, for better or worse.

We never talked about faith back in those days, but she still taught me something of Jesus' love for us. On a cosmic scale, we all have reason to be depressed. We're unworthy of God's perfect love in our sin and shame. We're unworthy of His affection and His attention. And if you read the Bible, you know that we've given God and all His many servants loads of reasons to break up with us for good. To end our second chances.

But then we see Jesus on the cross, suffering and dying for us.

When I was cutting myself, I imagined that shedding my own blood could somehow save me. Through her own sacrifice, Wendy mirrored a much greater truth: We're not saved by our own blood but by someone else's. We're saved through love—not the emotion, but the decision.

The third element that pulled me out of that depressive episode grew out of both of these. And it came in, what seemed at the time, the form of utter disaster.

It came upon us as our junior year of college was coming to a close. We were making plans for real adulthood. Marriage was a possibility but not a certainty. I was already excited about taking a trip to Britain and Ireland with some fellow English majors the following winter and was plotting my future as a bestselling novelist. And if I *had* to work a normal job for a couple of years before someone noticed my genius, so be it.

When Wendy told me that she was late, I didn't panic. It had to be just a normal fluctuation in her period, I figured. But we were heading into finals, and neither of us needed the distraction. So we went to a local pregnancy clinic for a test.

I remember the room—white and blue with crouched tables

and, oddly, children's books. As we waited, Wendy and I sat, hand in hand. The clinician—young, brown hair, wearing glasses—sat down beside us. Surely she knew, just by looking at us, what we wanted the answer to be. But she was a pro: no pitying looks, no apologies. She said, simply, that the test was positive.

I felt the nausea sweep in. "How . . . " I remember asking after a beat or two, "how reliable are those tests? Could there be some mistake?"

With a couple of words of explanation, she told us there was no mistake. She gently gave us some pamphlets—information on every option and eventuality—and walked out to give us some space.

Wendy started to cry before the door closed.

We went back to my apartment and sat on my beat-up couch. She cried. I might have too. And then, after ten minutes or so, we realized we needed to make plans. We needed to figure out what to do.

My brain screamed that I wanted this situation to be gone. All my hopes for myself, all my plans, were imperiled. I was terrified of the consequences that were waiting around the corner.

Growing up, my political cartoonist father had spoken at dozens of Right-to-Life conventions, had drawn up hundreds of pro-life cartoons. And even as I began to question some of his other beliefs and opinions—pushing against them and sometimes arguing strenuously with him—in this my dad and I were in lockstep. Abortion was wrong. It was evil. But only by making this baby go away could I save myself. One tiny procedure, and Wendy and I would have our lives back. We could keep on the same track. And most importantly, our parents would never need to know.

Every part of me believed that abortion was a terrible, tragic act. But if Wendy had opened that door, I wouldn't have fought it. I imagined how sad I'd feel, and how that sadness would cover over an inevitable sense of relief.

But abortion wasn't an option for her—not in a million years. And even though she herself was adopted, Wendy couldn't imagine carrying a baby to term and then giving it up. No, she was going to keep the baby, no matter the cost.

Love—love as a decision—visited my miserable little living room, where on that miserable little couch sat two miserable little people.

I got up, walked to the kitchen, reached in a drawer, and pulled out a green, paper-coated twist tie—the kind you wrap around your bread bag to keep the bread from getting dry. I fashioned it into a little ring, went back into the living room and bent my knee.

"Wendy," I said, tears leaking out of the corners of my eyes, "will you marry me?"

She said yes, and we smiled through our tears, and I tried to swallow the terror in my throat.

I've written about the immediate aftermath of that moment before, so I won't revisit that in detail now. I'll just say that the calls we made to our parents a few minutes later were just as horrible as I'd expected they'd be. The hurt, the shame, the anger . . . it was all there. Worse than I'd imagined it would or even could be. Even now, when I talk about it—think about it—it makes me want to cry.

You'd think that, if a little bullying in third grade or a strong infatuation was enough to send me spiraling out of control, an actual crisis would be enough to make my brain spontaneously combust. But curiously, that didn't happen.

Oh, I was freaked. The terror and shame I felt was quite real and, at times, quite powerful. While Wendy's and my parents rallied beside us after the initial shock, and while our friends were helpful in our pushing forward, the months leading up to the wedding were hard. I was grieving, really—saying goodbye, forever, to the life I had imagined for myself and all of its myriad possibilities. The future felt stranger and smaller. I felt like part of me was about to die: My single self was standing in front of the firing squad, smoking his last cigarette. And part of me wanted that cigarette to last forever, because I just wasn't ready.

But here's the thing: All this sadness, all this terror, made sense. It wasn't fun, but it wasn't the static of depression, either, the melancholy of unmoored mental illness. I wasn't torturing myself with anxieties and self-doubts—imagined shadows of what might be or what might come. This crisis was real and tangible. Like a cut, this pain was something I could understand. It pushed me out of my passivity and into action. I couldn't lie in bed and feel sorry for myself in the face of this crisis: I had to *do* something.

It doesn't work that way for everybody, of course. For many, I'd imagine, real-world crises are more likely to trigger depression than alleviate it. But depression itself is, in a way, a lot like cutting: It has a lot more to do with what's inside us than what happens to us outside. The first depressive episode most folks get is *caused* by something: We can point to what started us down this path. But the more depressive episodes you have, the smaller the triggers become. Sometimes those suffering can't point to a trigger at all. It's almost like the first episode is like a broken arm, while the fourth is like catching the flu. You know how you suffered the break. But the virus? It probably snuck up on you without warning, from one of the countless people you talked with or the countless things you touched.

But while depressive triggers can be mysterious and incredibly varied, I think many depressive episodes—or at least those I've gone through—share something in common: a sense of futility and helplessness. It's like we're slipping down an icy hill, powerless to stop ourselves or steer clear of others. And the depression inside us whispers that it's futile or pointless to even try.

Depression lies a lot.

Who cares? depression tells us. *Who cares about you? Why should you care about anyone?*

Finding a reason to care is like finding a set of spikes on that icy hill. And when Colin came around—when I had a wife and a son who were depending on me—I found that reason to care.

For years, I'd been crushed by sin and shame. For years, I felt the weight of my worthlessness—that I had forsaken the lessons of my parents and turned my back on my God. For me, an unexpected pregnancy was a worst-case scenario—the annihilation of the facade, the exposure of the self I so rigorously protected. The walls of my Jericho had fallen with a trumpet blast.

But freedom comes with the loss of a lie. And even as bad as I felt, I wasn't pretending anymore. And as the weeks went on, part of me began to see I wasn't just dying to one sort of life; I was being born into another. I was forced into a place of not just wishing for a bright future, but also building one—not just for myself, but for others as well. I didn't have the luxury of unmoored misery anymore. I needed to cowboy up.

And when the wedding was over, I experienced something I'd not truly felt for years: hope.

A few weeks later, I woke up at 3 a.m., groggy but excited. Wendy and I drove up I-25 from Colorado Springs to the farmhouse near Longmont, where Wendy's family lived. Her dad and I loaded her stuff in the car—the belongings with which we'd fill our new apartment in Hastings.

Our apartment.

We pulled away and headed east, where the gray sky was

just beginning to glow with the coming dawn. In the quiet of that morning, as we held hands in the car, I was as happy as I'd ever been.

Of course by now you know something else came along for the ride too.

CHAPTER 5

GUT CHECK

Monsters are real, and ghosts are real too.
They live inside us, and sometimes, they win.

STEPHEN KING, *The Shining*

IN A POP CULTURE ENAMORED of happy endings, the previous chapter should've been the end of the book, or the last scene in a movie right before the credits roll: The self-obsessed lead character discovers the real meaning of love, and he and his bride drive into a bright, new morning. The end. Thanks for coming.

But you know what our culture likes even more than happy endings? Sequels. These days, any movie that makes enough to cover its catering costs gets a sequel.

Sequels are particularly popular in horror franchises. *Halloween*'s Michael Myers and *Friday the 13th*'s Jason have both had more comebacks than John Elway. Every movie, it looks like these bogeymen are well and truly dead—shot or stabbed or eaten by sharks, maybe (I'm not a big expert in slasher movies). And then somehow, they come back. Even though, generally speaking, each new sequel is worse than the one before.*

Depression shares a lot in common with horror-movie sequels. Just when you think you're on your way to a happily-ever-after sort of life, it can come back. Not always, but sometimes. Experts say that of the people who suffer from depression, about half will suffer at least one relapse in their lives.[1] And for those who suffer from two or three serious depressive episodes, the chances rise that their depression will think that it's the mental-illness equivalent of Michael Myers: It'll likely be back to harass some more, or at least try. Some people, due to a complex and imperfectly understood stew of biology and circumstance and who knows what else, are prone to depression. Experts say that, for some people who make the trip to mental illness, it's less a one-time ticket to Depressionville and more a lifetime punch card. "In many cases, depression is a chronic or recurring disease, and as such, it is best managed like a chronic illness," write doctors Jürgen Unützer and Mijung Park for *Primary Care* in 2012.[2]

Like those subpar horror sequels, depressive recurrences get progressively harder to wade through. And unlike a movie, you can't just stand up and leave.

For those who've suffered through acute depression, that thought can be, well, pretty depressing. You struggle through the sadness, the sense of worthlessness, the sleeplessness, the numbness and come out of the experience alive, wiser, and stronger. But when it attacks a second, a third, an *eighth* time, it can push many to despair. And as I mentioned in the previous chapter, while there's often a trigger or trauma that you can point to following your first depressive episode, subsequent ones can come without

---

* Example 1A: *Jaws 3 in 3-D*. "This time, it's personal."

much reason at all.[3] You can feel as though you'll never be "normal." And the threat of continued or repeated abnormality can be devastating.

"Dearest, I feel certain that I'm going mad again," wrote author Virginia Woolf (whom modern scholars believe suffered from manic-depression) in her suicide note. "I feel we can't go through another of those terrible times."[4]

Woolf died in 1941, when the treatment of mental illness was, if not in its infancy, at least in clinical preschool. And while we still have much to learn about what mental illness even is, let alone how to treat it, I'd like to think that people who might've despaired in Woolf's day could've been saved today.

But depression isn't like polio, vanquished with a vaccine. Even with all the tools of modern science and psychology in our reach, even with our formidable array of treatment options, depression haunts us still. And while we can often get rid of it once and for all, sometimes it hides in the cellar of our minds, waiting and watching.

It's like the old radio drama "Sorry, Wrong Number"* or any variety of slasher flicks, where the killer's in the house the whole time.

Colin's coming seemed to cure my depression. Yes, I was scared to death about being a father. And when he finally came into the world, I felt like the hospital was being incredibly irresponsible in kicking us out after just a day without so much as an instruction manual. Lego sets sometimes come with instruction books as thick as your thumb, and here, the doctors were trusting us with a living

---

* Haven't heard it? Search for it on YouTube. You can listen to the Agnes Moorehead original there. It's so good, people.

being offering only a *flimsy little pamphlet*? What is this, IKEA? And we're supposed to be managing with this squirming, squalling thing for eighteen to twenty-two years?! Someone needs to look into this *parenting* thing a little bit deeper.

But I didn't have much time to think about it all. I had way too many diapers to change and classes to take and résumés to write and pureed turnips to stuff into the little guy's face. Every day was a whirlwind of crises and plans, little domestic joys and minor panic attacks. And in Hastings—still in college—by the time we put Colin down for the night, I was too exhausted to be depressed. Sure, I lost sleep—but only because our baby was a howling child of the night—up and ready to go at 8 p.m., ready to sleep by 2 or 3 a.m. (We called him our little vampire baby.) The suicidal ideation I experienced throughout much of college disappeared almost completely—and stayed dormant for years.

The situations that seemed to trigger the (still as-of-yet undiagnosed) depression and anxiety in me before didn't seem to be triggers anymore. Wendy and I moved from Hastings back to Colorado Springs and hopped from apartment to apartment to house to house, and I was just fine. Family life proved to be pretty great—so much so that Wendy and I decided to have another baby, this time *on purpose*. Our daughter, Emily, came along, and while she might've technically been louder than Colin, she slept through the night better.

I was living the life mostly seen in 1950s family shows: I had a wife, two kids, and a dog. Only difference was Wendy had a job, too, and it always paid more than mine did. I felt normal. Moreover, I felt happy.

And then . . . I wasn't.

I was working for the Professional Rodeo Cowboys Association at the time—a strange fit for someone who'd only been on a horse twice. But small newspapers didn't pay much, and the big ones weren't interested in me yet. The PRCA needed someone to write press releases for them, and eventually that evolved into a job editing its trade publication, the *ProRodeo Sports News*.

I was, as they'd say in the rodeo biz, a greenhorn. Most of the folks I worked with had lived around horses and cattle most of their lives. My only familiarity with cows was from the fast-food hamburgers I stuffed in my face. (I'm assuming some of it was beef, anyway.) When I wore a cowboy hat for the first time, our department's sage administrative assistant—we called her Queen, and with reason—looked at me in horror. "You take that off right now!" she told me. The brim, she said, looked like the hat came right out of the box (which it had), and she was determined to shape it so I'd not be laughed at. (Rodeo, believe it or not, is very fashion forward.)

And while I never rode a horse very well, I grew to understand the difference between bull riding and bulldogging, what made for a high-scoring saddle bronc ride, and could rattle off the names of the best bucking bulls in pro rodeo history. I grew to love the sport.

The editor part of the gig was a bigger challenge than the rodeo part.

It wasn't the first time I'd been the "boss." I'd been an editor before. But it was the first time that most of the folks I was supervising were older and, in terms of rodeo at least, much smarter than I was. I was all of twenty-six. My handful of employees were mostly in their thirties and forties. I felt like a new swimmer who'd just lost his water wings, but instead of being given the chance to flail around the pool a little, I'd been tossed into the Pacific.

It was my first real experience with middle management, too, with pressures both above and below. My supervisor told me everyone had to work from 8 to 5. I had an employee who had to pick up her kids at 4. She'd come in at least an hour early, and she never missed a deadline. But to my boss, all that was beside the point. See, he had bosses to answer to as well.

And then there was this, too: I really liked to be liked. I wanted to be more than a good boss: I wanted to be the *cool* boss. I didn't necessarily want to go to the bar or play poker with everyone, but I wanted to be *asked* to go to the bar or play poker, y'know?

But let's be honest: When you're scared of horses and a kindly administrative assistant has to make sure you've got your hat brim in the right shape, you're seriously far from cool in the world of rodeo.

So I leaned on what got me the promotion in the first place: hard work. Lots of it. I started spending sixty, seventy, even eighty hours at the office, trying to lasso the elements of my life that I could control, hoping that'd somehow help me feel better about the parts I couldn't.

But that came with a price, too. The more time I spent at work, the less I spent with my family. Emily was pretty little then, and I missed or barely remember a lot of those special moments that parents are supposed to be around for. I was too busy writing about bareback riders and tie-down ropers and what makes the Calgary Stampede unique. "When people are on their deathbed, no one ever regrets spending too much time with their children," a coworker once told me. She was right—even at the time I knew it—but I couldn't stop. Work wasn't an addiction, exactly, but it was a compulsion, a salve. And the more time I spent away from home, the guiltier I felt. And the guiltier I felt, the more I worked to make myself feel better.

(*"Why are you working?" demanded the little prince.*

"So that I may forget," replied the editor . . .)

I felt like I was failing at work and failing at home. Was I growing more depressed because I was failing? Or did I feel like a failure because of my depression? These are not easy questions to parse, but I knew I was slipping into an uneasy, and unhealthy, state of mind.

The suicidal ideation came back gradually—so gradually I scarcely noticed it. Thinking about dying became almost a lullaby for me: I'd plan my own demise as I slowly fell asleep. I was functional, but I was rarely happy by then. With few exceptions, my moods had been winnowed down to (a) slightly miserable, or (b) unconscious.

I wished life worked more like a video game. After all, if a game grew too frustrating, it was a simple matter to just press the reset button. Why couldn't life come with one of those? Something you could press to start your existence from your last good save point, redo the errors of your last session, and move on to a better place? But God didn't give us such a thing. We control our own lives, and if we take a wrong turn in the dungeon, we can't start over. We can only push on or press off. And just contemplating some sort of "off" button in my life—the idea of stepping away from life's game and moving on to . . . well, something else . . . was relaxing. Heaven wasn't something I hoped for. All I wanted was a little peace—a place soft and warm where I could pull the darkness over my head like a sheet.

But even with all those warning signs, what happened next was a complete shock.

Around 3 a.m., I woke up as a wave of nausea hit me. I felt it in my gut, my throat, my cheeks. I dashed to the bathroom.

But nothing happened. As I knelt by the toilet, nothing came.

But when I stood back up, it felt like a large, disgusting explosion was imminent.

Remember the Winnie-the-Pooh story when Pooh eats too much honey at Rabbit's house, tries to leave, and then gets stuck in Rabbit's front door? He can't go forward, he can't go back? Sorry to ruin that story for you now, but the gunk in my gut felt like it was playing Winnie-the-Pooh. It wouldn't come up, it wouldn't go back, and all I could do was wait for it.

When mental health experts look for signs of depression or anxiety in kids, they're not just looking for telltale *emotional* signals—sadness, irritability, suicidal feelings, and the like. Often, mental illness manifests in very physical ailments. Children might complain of headaches that never get better with aspirin or stomachaches with no discernable cause. Because children often can't articulate or even pinpoint serious mental angst, and because the adults in their midst often brush off these sorts of emotional complaints with a smile and a wave of the hand, these physical ailments can form an important tell for anxiety and depression.

I think I mentioned the night I freaked out when I was supposed to officially join the family church—when my parents thought that perhaps I'd changed my mind and became a Taoist. I had a lot of stomach ailments back then, it seems. I think back to all the school I missed in junior high. Makes me wonder whether my body was trying to tell me something.

The physical problems don't vanish when those depressed kids become depressed adults. Our psychology and physiology are deeply and inescapably connected: Physical problems can cause real psychological anguish, and depression doesn't always manifest itself most obviously in crying jags or suicidal thoughts. Sometimes it's the headache that just won't go away, or the literal pain in the neck that no amount of rubbing will completely alleviate, or the cramps and queasiness we feel at the most inopportune moments.

Stress often manifested itself with physical symptoms for me, and they continued through college and into my working career. But these stomach woes, as annoying as they were, were tolerable—frequent, but not constant. My stomach would turn cranky for a day or two and then settle back down for a couple of weeks or a month. Rarely, if ever, did I miss work because my stomach felt like a wad of paper clenched and squeezed in some oversized fist. I was used to it.

But this time, it felt different.

Thankfully, my wife and I had just finished the basement in our house, and because we didn't know what we were doing, we made the bathroom huge—so much so that a full-grown man could lie right on the floor. (The walls were also a nice, fitting shade of salmon—not quite the hue of a certain stomach analgesic, but not far off. It was as if the decor itself was trying to settle my tum-tum.) So, after I was relatively sure the stomach could make the trip downstairs, I grabbed a pillow and a couple of blankets and parked myself on that cold bathroom floor.

I barely left the basement for the next three weeks.

At least the couch was comfortable.

Cowboy up.

I've mentioned the phrase before. It's the marching cry of every rodeo cowboy—the rural American equivalent of "Keep calm and carry on." You push through adversity. You don't let your bumps and bruises and broken bones keep you from tightening your bull rope around a 2,000-pound monster of spinning, bucking beef.

Deb Greenough, a hall-of-fame bareback rider, used to show kids his "Popeye" muscle—a bicep that had torn away from his bone and reattached itself lower down on his arm. He could've had surgery and repaired the thing properly, but it would've meant being sidelined for several months. Instead, he took six weeks off and returned to the arena. The next year, he became a world champion.

Robert Etbauer, a two-time saddle bronc champ, once lost his thumb during a bronc ride gone bad. He was hanging off the side of the horse, hands dragging along the ground, when the bronc stepped on his thumb and popped it right off. After he finally freed himself, he walked around the arena til he found his missing digit, picked it up and walked out—finally making his way to the hospital where doctors successfully reattached it. When I asked him about how he had the presence of mind to coolly pluck his thumb and brush it free of the rodeo dirt, the soft-spoken cowboy looked at me as if it was the dumbest question he's ever been asked in his life.

"What was I going to do?" he said with a half smile. "Sit down in the dirt and cry?"

Cowboy up.

Many people deal with life's problems, including some manifestations of depression, by cowboying up. If you're thrown, you pick yourself up and move on—picking up any stray fingers that may have popped off in the process. You power through. You don't feel sorry for yourself. You don't sit down and cry.

That's how I learned to deal with my college-age depression after my other stint in bed, staring at the ceiling. I wasn't happy, exactly, but I pushed through. I went to class, took my tests, hung out with Wendy and my friends when I could, and slowly, I crept out of it—at least enough to enjoy myself every now and then. At least enough to feel like I was a participant my own life. I struggled with a lot of stuff, true, but I cowboyed up. And then, suddenly, I had a wife, two kids, and a career to pursue. I had stories to write and bills to pay. I was living and moving forward, and that forward momentum kept me stable and sane.

The philosophy of Cowboy Up served me well.

But sometimes you can't. And sometimes, honestly, you shouldn't. To just ignore the signs of depression—to push through as if they weren't there—can sometimes work for a while. But they call it *mental illness* for a reason. Sometimes it's like a cold and you get over it. But sometimes it's like cancer. It won't go away on its own. And if you let it go, the consequences could be dire.

Or, to stick with a more rodeo-centric analogy, sometimes people get thrown by depression—bucked off and thrown to the dirt. Sometimes that depression's like a horse that, for whatever reason, got a little spooked and didn't want you on its back anymore. Every rider gets thrown now and then. But as long as no permanent damage was done, you just get back up, brush off the dirt, and ride again. You get back on the horse. You have to.

But sometimes, depression's like 2,000 pounds of spinning, bucking bull. And if you're not careful, it could kill you.

Bodacious was already one of the most feared bovines in rodeo history. He was fast and strong and, even before he became the most feared bull in rodeo history, was almost impossible to ride. But in 1995, like a pitcher mastering a nasty slider, Bodacious developed a new move—almost a hiccup in his buck. He'd come out of the gate with a fairly typical buck and spin, and the bull's momentum would yank the cowboy's head and torso down toward the bull's back. But then, the bull would take a rapid, unexpected *second* buck—sending his head *up* just as the momentum of the first was pulling the cowboy *down*. And with this second move, Bodacious moved from being just a fearsome challenge for the world's best bull riders to wet-your-pants terrifying.

In 1995, during the Pro Bull Riding Finals, legendary bull rider Tuff Hedeman drew Bodacious. He took Bodacious's first move just fine. Then the bull whipped his head up like a catapult and smashed it straight into Hedeman's face. He "bounced off the bull's back like a rag doll," according to a piece in the *New Yorker*.[5] I wasn't there, but someone who was told me later that it looked like Hedeman's face had been smashed a full two inches into his skull.

Doctors said that every bone in his face had been broken. It took thirteen and a half hours of reconstructive surgery and five titanium plates to put Hedeman back together.

Cowboy up? Hedeman did. He was competing at the National Finals Rodeo (NFR) two months later. He rode several bulls successfully, and many said it was a testament to the guy's courage that he was out there at all.

But Hedeman's tenacious and tough, not dumb. When he drew Bodacious again, he let the bull win. He wasn't allowed to forfeit, but instead of pulling his rope tight around the bull's middle and hanging on for dear life, he hung onto the back of the chute—letting the bull charge into the arena without a rider and taking a zero for the round.

When another cowboy drew Bodacious later during the NFR, he wore a protective hockey mask. And the bull *still* shattered his cheek and eye socket. Sammy Andrews, the bull's owner, retired Bodacious the next night. The animal, he said, was just too dangerous.

The ability to cowboy up can get you through a lot of things. But you can't be stupid about it. Sometimes, you've got to stop— or your depression will force you to anyway.

For several years I'd followed, in my own quiet, desk-jockey sort of way, that mantra of cowboy up. As my stress level rose and my sense of failure grew, I kept on moving. I'd go to work every day, pushing through my eight, twelve, fourteen hours of human resources headaches and deadlines. As my stomach clenched and cramped, I adapted to its patterns and pushed through.

But that morning when I woke up at 3 a.m. and lay down on my bathroom floor, deadlines or no, I knew I couldn't make it into work. I couldn't make it to the car. And while my most obvious and crippling symptom was the nausea, I soon realized that I was sick with more than a stomach bug. It wasn't that I just couldn't eat; I couldn't do *anything*.

For three weeks, I spent about twenty-three and a half hours a day on that couch in the basement. Sometimes I tried to read, but I couldn't focus. Sometimes I'd try to watch TV, but it made me nauseous. Most nights, I found I could stomach the Disney Channel at around 2 a.m., when I'd typically wake up and stay awake for the rest of the night. Every three or four days, I'd drag myself into the shower and run water over my body, rubbing the soap over me slowly, slowly, to try to wipe away the stench of myself. And occasionally, when everyone else had gone to work or school, I'd even crawl up the stairs—literally crawling, some afternoons—and eat a cracker or two. I dared not come up when anyone was home, so sick I felt and so ashamed I was of this weird, helpless thing I'd become.

One day, Wendy sent Colin and Emily down the stairs for a visit—hoping, perhaps, to remind me that I had a life outside the basement, that subterranean pit I was wallowing in. I looked at them, standing in front of me, uncomfortable and unsure, and I burst into tears.

Sometimes, I wondered if I was dying.

It was my stomach. That's what I told everybody, and that was at least partly true: I felt sick all the time. I lost twenty pounds in three weeks.

But I also knew that my gut wasn't the root of what was wrong with me. It was just the most noticeable symptom. I was simply . . . broken. Something in my mind had reared up and smashed my face in. I couldn't cowboy up. I could barely climb the stairs. And I wondered whether I'd ever leave the basement again.

Severe depression is, by definition, an unhealthy, unnatural state of mind, inherently and wholly illogical. It really and truly doesn't make sense. And that's what makes it so difficult for those who've never dealt with it (and even many who have) to understand. *Cheer up*, people say. *Get out. Get active. Life's not so bad.* And, of course, they're right. On some level, you *know* they're right. This is exactly how you should be thinking and what you should be doing, because this is what normal people think and do.

But let's face it: When you're dealing with depression, you're not normal. In fact, you're a wee bit insane. You might not be talking to lamps or calling yourself the Queen of England, but your brain is a little warped. What makes logical sense to everyone else—what makes logical sense to you, very often—just doesn't compute somehow. Telling someone suffering from severe depression to cheer up is a little like telling someone with a shattered leg to take a quick jog around the park.

But unlike broken bones, which are obvious to everybody, your broken brain is out of view. It doesn't even have the decency to come with a telltale cough or fever. You can complain about the pain, but no one can see any real reason why you should be in any. And unless you're aware that you have depression, *you* don't see why you should be in pain, either. You just know that you are.

At the time, I didn't know I was depressed. I just knew that I was, without warning, unable to cope with life's simplest challenges. That almost everything I saw, heard, or felt was making me sick. It didn't make sense. But depression's inherent illogic didn't make it any easier to deal with. You feel like the way you feel now will be the way you will feel always and forever.

And in the absence of treatment, there's some truth to that. You have to find a way to move forward, and both counseling and medication can be incredibly useful to facilitate that. There's no replacement for expert help.

I didn't get psychiatric help then. I didn't know I needed it. But I did get help. I was fortunate that I had people in my life who helped me push forward. And as happened in college, they gave me the gift of three key elements. They happened pretty much simultaneously. But for the sake of clarity, let me talk about them one at a time.

Time. The miracle of our creation is found not only in how we're made, but also in how we can—slowly, painfully—be remade. When man-made things break, they are broken. If they're going to get fixed, someone's going to have to fix 'em. But when people break, we can heal. Cuts stitch themselves together. Broken bones mend. As Deb Greenough taught me, even a bicep torn away from the scapula can, given time, reattach. We may be left with scabs or scars, but we can be whole again. And sometimes, we can feel stronger than before.

And even when our mind breaks a little, it, too, can heal. Not always, and not always perfectly, but most of us can find a way to move on. When we grieve over the loss of someone we love, we sometimes feel we'll never get over it. But usually we do. We always feel the pain of the loss, but with that pain comes a hint of gratitude: Even the pain reminds us how wonderful it was to have known and loved that person, even if it wasn't long enough. When we suffer losses of a different kind—a friendship or a job, or when we deal with financial or personal setbacks—we often learn lessons and use them to move forward with a little more wisdom. Our physical, emotional, and spiritual wounds sometimes leave us with a limp. But we can still walk. We can still move forward . . . with time.

The time I spent on that couch wasn't a particularly productive time—not unless there's some benefit of watching a lot of innocuous *Mickey Mouse Club* reruns that I'm not aware of. But I think I needed it. I needed the time to see that even if I fell apart for a while, the world wouldn't. I still took in breath. I could still feel my heart beat inside me.

And even as I wondered whether I could be dying, I realized one day that I didn't want to. Sure, I still sometimes wished for that reset button, but the off button wasn't a desirable option for me anymore. In time, I came to see time itself—the time we're given in our bodies, in this world—as a gift, even if it was a gift I wasn't making particularly good use of. Even wasting that time on that cursed couch was a better alternative than *not* being on that cursed couch.

I wanted to be here, and be *me*. Slowly, my desire to breathe returned, inch by inch. My interest in the things of this world grew bit by bit.

Let me stress that coming out of a depressive state is a long and gradual one. Just as I didn't start being depressed all of a sudden, I wasn't miraculously better after three weeks on that couch—ready to celebrate and maybe paint the house. For months afterward, I wasn't quite myself. My stomach still gave me fits for a while. I still wanted to sleep a lot, and dealing with people took a ton out of me. But over weeks and months, I remembered where I had been and saw where I was now, and I knew that I was getting better.

But it wasn't just time that did it. I had help.

Love. Even if we've never cracked open a Bible, most of us know evangelical America's favorite verse, John 3:16. *For God so loved the world, that he gave his only Son, that whoever believes in him should not perish but have eternal life.*

The verse sums up the essence of Christianity. But it's so familiar to us that we sometimes lose the backstory.

For God so loved the world, we're told. And so He gave us His son. Why did He need to give us Jesus? *Because we needed Him.* It wasn't that we deserved that special gift of life and salvation. Just the opposite, really. He loved us not because we showed a great deal of love for Him, following His commandments and all, but *in spite* of what we do. He loved us, and because God also knew how broken we all were, He sent His Son so that we could be with Him anyway. God's love isn't dependent on what we can do for Him. He loves us.

That's what real love is. I learned this from Wendy earlier, but I'd forgotten it again. In fact, I forget it occasionally even now. Somewhere, somehow, I—like most of America—learned a lie, that the amount that we're loved is dependent on the value we bring to the party. We've defined love in capitalistic terms—that our inherent worth is predicated on our skills and talents and dedication, and our ability to love in return. It's the old concept of supply and demand. If we supply what people want and need, then we'll be in demand. We'll be loved. But God doesn't work that way. He doesn't give us what we deserve. He gives us what we need. He blesses us, and often beyond measure.

I think God's love works a little like the biblical story of the coin in the fish's mouth we read about in Matthew 17. In the story, we're told that Peter tells Jesus that they owe a temple tax. Jesus says they don't really need to pay the tax, but so as "not to give offense," He tells Peter to go down to the lake and catch a fish; it'll have the necessary tax money in its mouth. And sure enough, the fish does.

Now, if Peter had been a richer fellow, this conversation never would've happened. Peter probably would've fished the money out of his own purse. But because he didn't have the money, he was witness to a little miracle.

That's the funny thing about God's love. We see it most clearly when we have nothing to give.

And sometimes, if we give the people around us a chance, they mirror that love for us.

I felt like I was failing everyone around me: my employers, my family, my friends. I wasn't supplying anything of value to the people I cared for. How could they care for me?

But they did.

My boss, instead of firing me, told me to take whatever time I needed to get better, smoothing things over with his own bosses and calculating the time, legally, I had available to me. I could use it up until the last second, he said, and after that we could talk again. My parents, who must've known that my sickness was more than just a stomach thing, fed me books—Christian books that stressed the love of God and the inherent value that He finds in us—and affirmation. Sure, I might've fallen for the moment. I wasn't all that they, or I, expected I would be. I don't know how disappointed they were about that, really, but for me, that sense of failure was pretty crushing. But their love never stopped. And even though I knew it wouldn't, to see that unconditional love in action changed the game.

And throughout it all, Wendy never failed to show me that she loved me—even though I'd essentially deserted her for the confines of the basement, forcing her into single motherhood for nearly a month.

But sometimes, even unconditional love comes with a responsibility that looks like a caveat.

Action. Wendy was great about showing me love and patience, both of which I most definitely needed. But after a few weeks, she came downstairs, saw my mopey self and ran her fingers through my hair.

"I don't know what to do," she said with the sweetest smile ever. "Part of me wants to give you a big hug and never let you go. And part of me wants to give you a kick in the butt."

Depression's a funny thing. Not everyone who suffers from it can hear those four words—*kick in the butt*—in the moment. But thankfully, I could. I knew that I was loved. Time had taken me as far as I could go. I needed to get off that couch. I needed that gentle kick.

I had my time. I felt the love around me. Now it was time to cowboy up.

In the end, everyone who's depressed—no matter how good his or her psychologist is or how effective the person's medicine is—needs to cowboy up, to move forward, even if they don't want to. You might not be able to do so initially, but you have to do it eventually. You need to start moving. And if someone gives you a little kick to get you on your way, be grateful. It may not come at the right time or be said in the right way, but you can find truth in those words.

Let's go back to Winnie-the-Pooh, when he was stuck in Rabbit's front door. He was stuck, no doubt about it. And I was too. But Christopher Robin knew how to get him out.

It would take time . . .

"A week!"said Pooh gloomily . . .

It would take love . . .

"Then would you read a Sustaining Book, such as would help and comfort a Wedged Bear in Great Tightness?" . . .

And eventually, it would take a mighty tug to get him unstuck.

And for a long time Pooh only said "Ow!" . . .

And "Oh!" . . .

And then, all of a sudden, he said "Pop!" just as if a cork were coming out of a bottle.

I needed time, love, and a little kick to get me unstuck. And when I, like Pooh, came tumbling out, I told myself that I'd do my best to keep from ever getting stuck again.

CHAPTER 6

SILENCE

The pupil dilates in darkness and in the end finds light,
just as the soul dilates in misfortune and in the end finds God.

VICTOR HUGO, *Les Misérables*

WHY?

Such a simple word, just three letters long. But when it comes
to things of the soul, few are more powerful. The word is imbued
with mystery and wonder and, sometimes, agony. And often,
when we ask why, we feel the ache.

Why did I not die at birth? says Job.

Why, what evil has he done? says Pilate.

My God, my God, why have you forsaken me? says the psalmist.
Says Jesus.

Journalists are taught to answer a series of questions: who,
what, when, where, and why. The first questions are not necessarily easy to answer. But they have relatively concrete answers
once we find them.

Joe Smith, 22, was killed yesterday near a Colorado Springs supermarket. Eyewitnesses say two gunmen opened fire and . . . In one sentence, we know the who (Joe Smith), the what (was killed), the when (yesterday), and the where (near a Colorado Springs supermarket). But . . . why? To answer that, we need to know Joe Smith and his killers. We need to know more about the circumstances and surroundings. Often, the question of "why" unfolds like a rose, with layers upon layers of answers the deeper you go. If you get the answer to one "why," you're suddenly given another. If four questions can be answered in a sentence, the fifth—to be answered well—needs a book.

I left the Professional Rodeo Cowboys Association several months after my three-week "illness" and went to work for *The Gazette*, Colorado Springs' daily paper. I hopped through a variety of gigs there for a few years before becoming the paper's religion reporter. I loved the job because I was able to park on the *why*. I could be incredibly nosy, unpacking the history and poetry of a person, talking openly and honestly about hopes and fears and pain in a way that maybe even their closest friends didn't or couldn't. I didn't just talk to Christians: People of all faiths were part of my beat, and selfishly that gave me the excuse to learn about other religions and contrast them with my own. *Why were you attracted to Buddhism? Why did you go to Mecca? If you were raised in the church, why did you leave the faith?* As I learned about their beliefs, I learned more about my own. And naturally, covering religion at a time when Colorado Springs was known as the evangelical Vatican, I spent quite a bit of time talking with those who shared my own faith, too, and the stories I followed gave me opportunities to examine its beauty, power, tensions, and failings. *Why did you give up a successful business to help India's Untouchables? Why don't you believe that gay people should be married? Why would you risk your life to bring Bibles to*

North Korea? Why, pastor, did you steal all that money from your own church?

But the stories that touched me the most were those that had no definable answer. *Why did God allow my daughter to die? My church to fail? Why did He steal my voice? Make me attracted to men? Why? Why?*

One afternoon early in my gig, I talked with a man dying from cancer. He'd once weighed 250 pounds, most of it muscle. He was said to have had a booming voice back in the day, when he was healthy, and he inspired instant respect—even fear—in the troubled, wayward teens he watched over in a home for at-risk youth. But by the time I talked with him, he weighed half that. He wore a coat and a sweater and a stocking hat to keep the chill off his emaciated form. He talked gently and cried often, and he joked with me near the end of the interview that he should pay me to come back every week as therapy. And while he'd lost much of his physical strength, he still had plenty where it really counts.

Toward the end of the interview, we talked about his prayer life, and he admitted to something I had never heard a Christian say out loud before: Sometimes, when he prayed—when he poured out his pain and fear to the Almighty One who heals all wounds, who dries all tears—he felt nothing but silence. Emptiness. As if his words went into the blackness of the cosmos, unheard and unheeded. In those moments he felt utterly alone, even abandoned. *Why?* he was asking. *Why doesn't God answer? Where did He go?*

My God, my God, why have You forsaken me?

My friend—I felt that I could call him that after our interview—said he didn't feel that darkness all the time. Sometimes his time in prayer was "beautiful," he said. But those times of emptiness were a grave and terrible mystery to him.

I remember it so well, perhaps, because I feel that same void sometimes. God can feel so far away, particularly when my depression sidles close. Some of that's my own fault: I don't think it's an accident that my worst depressive episodes coincided with times when my faith life was essentially fallow.

But to blame depression on a weak faith is too simple an answer to the important question of *why*. Thousands, perhaps millions, of people with a faith much deeper and stronger than my own struggle with depression. They struggle to make sense of their despair, to find hope when all feels hopeless. They seek the face of God and find only darkness. They pray and in return hear silence.

Most of us know who Mother Teresa is. She spent decades serving God and helping the poor, and she became for many a model of Christian sacrifice and service. In 1979, Mother Teresa won the Nobel Peace Prize. But some of her private letters, particularly the ones she wrote to Jesus alone, show a side of the Catholic saint (she was canonized in 2016) that few ever suspected—a side troubled by doubt and depression for most of her life.[1]

In one letter to Jesus written in 1959, several years after she founded the Missionaries of Charity, she wrote this:

> They say people in hell suffer eternal pain because of
> the loss of God. . . . In my soul I feel just that terrible
> pain of loss, of God not wanting me, of God not being
> God, of God not really existing (Jesus, please forgive my
> blasphemies, I have been told to write everything). That
> darkness that surrounds me on all sides. I can't lift my
> soul to God—no light or inspiration enters my soul.[2]

In this affliction of ours, we keep good company. Even the best of us ask why.

When I began this book, I mentioned that faith can be a mighty bulwark against depression. It offers both purpose and hope: purpose, in the understanding that your life has meaning (even if it's not particularly wonderful for us all the time); hope, in that we serve a God who is the source of all hope. As awful and bleak as things get, we Christians are told that in the very end, things will be okay. Jesus told us, "In this world you will have trouble. But take heart! I have overcome the world" (John 16:33, NIV).

Fewer people believe that now, though. And I, for one, think it shows.

On October 17, 2019, two very different studies were released. The first, from the Pew Research Center, found that the United States is losing its religion. About 65 percent of us say that we're Christian—down a full 12 percentage points from just a decade earlier. In the same time frame, rates of people who don't believe in anything—classified as atheists, agnostics, or folks who just don't care that much—went from 17 percent to 26 percent. And the younger you are, the less likely you are to believe.[3]

The second study released that day came from the US Centers for Disease Control and Prevention. Researchers found that, while suicide rates continue to rise among all age groups, it's skyrocketing for youth. Suicide rates for Americans between ages ten and twenty-four rose a staggering 56 percent in a ten-year period (between 2007 and 2017).[4] "When a leading cause of death among our youth is increasing," statistician Sally Curtin told the *Wall Street Journal*, "it behooves all of us to pay attention and figure out what's going on."[5] When CBS News asked experts that all-important "why" question, those experts said a number of factors likely played a role, from our increasingly agitated society to growing stress in the lives of youth.[6] They mentioned that rates of depression have also been rising, almost in lockstep with suicide.[7]

I'm sure those experts are right. But as a layman, I have to wonder whether, in losing our religion, we're losing something else: the purpose and hope that come with it.

But as my own story suggests, let's not imagine that religion is some sort of cure-all for mental illness—a spiritual aspirin you can take two of and watch your depression go away. Yes, scads of studies show that the more religious people are, the fewer depressive symptoms they'll tend to have. But it's not so simple. According to the experts, the vision of God that I was given as a six-year-old Baptist—that of a God who would welcome me into heaven as long as I was crucified beforehand—is not particularly conducive to mental health. Likewise a concept of God that's less loving Father and more strict, angry judge. "If you tend to see God as punitive, threatening or unreliable, then that's not very helpful," Kenneth Pargament, a professor of psychology at Bowling Green State University, told *Live Science* in 2015.[8]

Sometimes, the triggers can be more complex. In a 2012 paper published in *Depression Research and Treatment*, researchers again confirmed that, generally, religious belief is good for depression.[9] But they noted that some studies found it depended, in part, on why people were suffering from depression in the first place. If a person of faith was dealing with depressive symptoms because of family issues—a fractured marriage, for instance, or trouble with their kids—their faith was less likely to help them. The authors suggested that because so many faith traditions place such a high value on marriage and family—raise your hands, evangelical Christians!—problems in those areas cut deeper. "Failure in family life, an area of particular importance to highly religious persons because of its emphasis by religious traditions, may predispose to higher levels of guilt and greater depression," the authors wrote.[10]

Guilt and shame, I know, are powerful depressive triggers. And sadly, depression itself can cause more guilt and shame. Many people—even people who suffer from depression—believe it's a sin. They *shouldn't* be depressed, they believe; it's a sign of mental or spiritual weakness. And so they don't share their struggles with the very community that should, as the Bible says, share his or her burdens. And even though depression is, by its very nature, a disease that isolates and separates its sufferers from community, there's a deeper tragedy sometimes at play in religious communities if the depression is particularly life-threatening. As articulated by Stephen H. Webb in the Catholic online journal *First Things*: "Anyone who even thinks about suicide typically feels deeply ashamed, but Christians in this situation have even more guilt heaped upon them due to the way suicide is usually treated as the gravest of sins."[11]

And then there are the silences.

I work with a lot of Christians—joyful, happy people who talk sincerely and fervently about what God is doing in their lives. They sometimes tell me how God "spoke" to them. In my home branch of Christianity, evangelicalism, it's trendy to talk about our union with God as a "relationship," with all that give-and-take intimacy the word implies, instead of a "religion."

But depression mutes our ability to have relationship with anyone, much less an unfathomably holy, literally untouchable God. And I wonder sometimes whether everyone perceives—or is supposed to perceive—God in the same way.

Long before I identified myself as depressed, I talked with a fellow Christian about how we each "knew" God. For him, knowing the Almighty seemed to come as easy to him as drinking coffee.

He felt God's presence everywhere—in church, in prayer, in song, and in silence.

I admitted that my experience was very different. I could count the times I felt God with me—powerfully, fully with me—on one hand. My relationship with God sometimes felt distinctly one-sided, I admitted: He felt less like a friend and more like a mysterious, awesome, indescribable *thing*—a being that I didn't as much *know* as I knew *about*. I believed in Him. I'd learn about Him in stories and sermons and songs and the Bible. But to *see* God, to *feel* Him, like we hear about in the worship songs, was as rare as a sighting of Bigfoot.

My friend told me that I was simply doing faith wrong. He doubted, in the end, whether I was even a Christian.

Was he right? Was I doing faith wrong? Or does my history of depression make it harder for me to feel the presence of God? Or does the Lord meet us all in different places? Is our relationship with Him—as ours is with all of our friends and family—a little different for each of us? He made us all unique. Would He not meet us all in unique ways?

I didn't—couldn't—articulate that to my friend then. Instead, I felt that familiar tang of shame and separation, that sense of failure in this, what I felt (Christian or no) was the most critical aspect of my existence. This person said that he doubted my faith. But I *did* have faith. I knew what I believed. I knew that, however mysterious and holy and untouchable God was to me, I still loved Him. So if (a) I loved God, but (b) my friend was right and I should be feeling more, what did that mean? Did that mean something inside me made it impossible to feel that love in return? That perhaps it wasn't enough to love Him? That there was a flaw in me that made me hard for *God* to love?

That's woefully theologically inaccurate, of course—just plain wrong. Nothing can separate us from the love of God, Paul told us in Romans 8:38-39. But I didn't know much about Scripture then, and my doubts of my own self-worth were pretty strong. And sometimes I wonder if other would-be Christians—folks who fill those "nones" columns today—got a gentle push in that direction from good Christians, well-meaning Christians, who think that faith is a cookie-cutter thing that looks the same for everyone.

Ironically, the Bible is filled with such imperfect believers—those who believed but felt, keenly, times of separation and depression.

"Even those people whose faith promises them that this will all be different in the next world cannot help experiencing anguish in this one," wrote Andrew Solomon in *The Noonday Demon*. And that is all too true. "Christ himself was the man of sorrows."[12]

As I was writing this very chapter, the senior pastor for my church began a series on the prophet Elijah—suggesting that even this mighty man of God suffered from depression.

He had lots of reasons to be depressed, of course. I've never had the queen of Israel plot to kill me.

Still, it's striking when you read 1 Kings 19:4.

> But he himself went a day's journey into the wilderness
> and came and sat down under a broom tree. And he asked
> that he might die, saying "It is enough; now, O Lord,
> take away my life, for I am no better than my fathers."

(It's also interesting that God walked Elijah through the same template that got me through my depressive episode when I was with the rodeo: time, love, and, frankly, a kick in the rear. God sent an angel to feed Elijah, sent him on a forty-day journey in the wilderness and—when Elijah still wasn't going anywhere but to the back of the cave—said, "What are you doing here, Elijah?" He then pushed him out to take care of some important business, which Elijah did, because even prophets need to cowboy up every now and again.)

He's not alone. Dealing with depression as I have, it's curiously heartening to read about how many of God's chosen have fought despair, hopelessness, and even thoughts of wanting to just be done with it all.

Jonah told God that it was "better for me to die than to live" (Jonah 4:3). Jeremiah is sometimes called the "weeping prophet" because of the misery he felt. Job, my favorite biblical depressive, "took a piece of broken pottery with which to scrape himself while he sat in the ashes" (Job 2:8). While lots of biblical commentators say all that scraping was meant to deal with the boils he was suffering with, the great nineteenth-century theologian Albert Barnes is one of several who suggest the scraping was meant also (in Barnes's words) to "'indicate' the greatness of his calamity and sorrow."[13] (When I read the passage, I can't help but be reminded of cutting.)

David wrote many an anguished psalm. Other psalmists poured out their hurt and sorrow to God (and everyone else) in their songs. In Psalm 73, Asaph sounds deeply self-pitying for much of it, and then writes what might sound to some a poetic description of depression and what it can do to us:

Thus my heart was grieved,
And I was vexed in my mind.
I was so foolish and ignorant;
I was like a beast before You.

PSALM 73:21-22, NKJV

But then Asaph turns around and says what we depressed Christians should always ultimately say:

> Nevertheless I am continually with You;
> You hold me by my right hand.
> You will guide me with Your counsel,
> And afterward receive me to glory.
>
> PSALM 73:23-24, NKJV

We can't know for certain that these characters suffered from depression. Obviously, no Old Testament psychiatrist spent a few hours with them and prescribed the BC equivalent of Zoloft. Still, these biblical characters, and many others, felt deep sorrow and anguish and sometimes even risked despairing of the very hope they were promised, and that they promised others. In spite of it all, they still followed. They still held on to hope, even if they didn't or couldn't feel it.

That's key: holding on to hope even when you can't feel it. It reminds me of one of my favorite passages in Annie Dillard's Pulitzer Prize–winning book, *Pilgrim at Tinker Creek.*

> Divinity is not playful. The universe was not made in jest
> but in solemn incomprehensible earnest. By a power that is
> unfathomably secret, and holy, and fleet. There is nothing
> to be done about it, but ignore it, or see. And then you
> walk fearlessly, eating what you must, growing wherever
> you can, like the monk on the road who knows precisely
> how vulnerable he is, who takes no comfort among death-
> forgetting men, and who carries his vision of vastness and
> might around in his tunic like a live coal which neither
> burns nor warms him, but with which he will not part.[14]

What we feel or don't, whether we hear God speak to us or not, it doesn't change the truth of faith, the reality of God and His unfathomably secret, holy power.

Why do we suffer from depression?

As we've seen, the answer—or rather, the answers—are complex. Each person's depression is a stew filled with all sorts of different ingredients: chemical, biological, environmental, circumstantial. Some people have lots of one sort of ingredient and less of another. Sometimes it can last for two weeks and never come back, and sometimes it can come and go, nearly at a whim, for decades. Some people respond well to one sort of treatment while others go completely unfazed. Doctors and psychologists can spend their lives studying the condition and still find more questions than answers.

But when you're a Christian, the question comes with an extra dollop of hurt and mystery. When we ask why we suffer from depression, what we're really asking sometimes is why God allowed me to suffer from it.

I don't have an answer for you. I'm no Old Testament prophet who knows the mind of God. I feel, keenly at times, the ache of that mystery. Your pastor—or your therapist or a theologian—may have a better answer for you. But let me offer you some thoughts I've gleaned from my own journey.

SIN AND SHAME

I know, I know, awkward. Talking about sin is very much out of favor in the culture today, and even we Christians sometimes dislike discussing it much. And I've spent pages reassuring you that depression—contrary to what some Christians may have told you—is not a sin.

But depression, I believe, can in some instances be a *by-product* of sin—not a punishment from God, exactly, but a punishment we subconsciously inflict on ourselves because we know we're out of alignment with Him.

About 2,500 years ago, the Greek philosopher Plato put forth a concept that modern philosophers call the theory of forms. Behind each "thing" we see on earth, be it a horse or a cat or an oak tree or whatnot, is an "ideal" representation of that form lurking somewhere in our psyche.[15] So when we look at an old, skinny horse, that ideal "form" we embrace informs our knowledge: We recognize the thing as a horse. But we also see how it deviates from that ideal form, so we can see, relative to that ideal, it's an old and skinny one. I think Plato was onto something. And I think that, if you'd allow me to stuff that bit of pagan philosophy into Christianity, there's something of the "ideal form" at work in all of us, too.

We are who we are, but we know we're not all that God designed us or wants us to be. God's original blueprints for each of us were unique, and each uniquely beautiful. God saw what each of us could be—our ideal form—and imbued us with a spark of that. And when God looks at us, I think He still sees all that beauty inside us, the creature He meant for us to be.

But sin—the world's sin and our own—twists that ideal and makes us who, on this earth, we really are. And because we understand dimly that the mortal reality of ourselves doesn't match the God-given design that still lurks deep down in us, we feel incredible dissonance: Who we are and who God designed us to be are so very, very different.

Back in college, I knew, deeply, that I wasn't the man God wanted me to be. My sin and dysfunction created a chasm between me and God. And if I'm being completely honest with myself, it often still does. From the outset of my depression, guilt and shame have been a big ingredient in my own stew. And sometimes, that guilt has a legitimate cause.

If you're depressed, I think this is where you have to start: Look at your life. Look at your behavior. Look at your sins—because, let's face it, we all have a few that we hold on to dearly, even if we try to hide them. And then deal with them. Confess them. Don't let them sit and chisel away at your ideal form. Naturally, the benefits to expunging what sin you can from your life go well beyond depression—and there's no guarantee that scouring off the sins in your life (let's not kid ourselves, an enormously difficult task, and one that you might have to repeat by the day or even hour) will cure or alleviate your depression. But it's one less trigger. One less reason to feel that sense of guilt and shame and worthlessness that I've found to be such a big part of my own depression.

But let me add a caveat: Sometimes we feel guilt or shame for things that aren't at all, or aren't precisely, sins.

Earlier in this chapter, I mentioned a study published in a 2012 issue of *Depression Research and Treatment*—one that found that people of faith sometimes were more prone to depression if they were depressed over family issues. We feel guilt over the wayward behavior of a son or daughter; we weren't good enough parents, or we did something horribly wrong. We can feel incredible shame if our marriage isn't picture perfect—if it's heading, perhaps, to divorce. When our families, these God-given institutions, fall outside our own ideal form for them, we feel that same sense of dissonance. We know something's not right. And because we're a part of those institutions—and they're a part of us—we don't just feel the pain inherent in the lies and the arguments and the sense that everything's crumbling in front of us: We blame ourselves that they're crumbling.

Sometimes we find (alas) that there's a kernel of truth to that. Or more than a kernel. But relational woes are rarely the product of one person, and we often take on way too much blame—especially, I think, if we're prone (or conditioned) to think we're bad people to begin with. We often take on responsibilities that aren't ours to take. And regardless of whether we're being fair to ourselves, the blame and guilt and shame we feel can pull us into the bowels of depression, making it ever so much harder for us to deal with the problems that caused it. Instead of the pain spurring us to action, it pulls us into a state of paralysis.

That's not helpful to anyone—not to your spouse, your children, certainly not to yourself. See, I believe that pain can be a gift from God: Whether it's physical, mental, or spiritual pain, it's meant to make us correct the things that hurt. But in the grip of depression, we lose our ability, and our will, to fix things.

Sometimes, I think, depression can be a way that we subconsciously punish ourselves—we toss ourselves into a dungeon we think we deserve and toss the key far, far away. But that, perhaps, shows a lack of faith in both the justice and the mercy of God. It's His responsibility to judge us—not ours. Our responsibility is to live our lives as best we can and reflect Christ in those lives to the best of our ability. Hard to do that when we've thrown ourselves into a dungeon.

One final word about sin and shame before we move on to the next point: That same 2012 paper mentioned that "a single study" found a higher disposition to depression in religious substance abusers. Addictions—be they to alcohol or drugs or porn or anything—are often thought by Christians to be sins or signs of weakness, even though scientific evidence stresses that addictions are diseases. Perhaps, when it comes to discussing the issue in the context of depression, it's almost beside the point as to which it is. The point is that addictions can go hand in hand with depression. Dealing with that addiction can, thus, address an aspect of that depression. Get help for that addiction—as painful as it might be to admit that you have one, as hard as it might be to quit. The only way the tippler from *The Little Prince* can stop being ashamed is if he stops drinking.

THE WILDERNESS

Let's go back to Elijah, during what my pastor would say was his big biblical depressive episode in 1 Kings 19. As soon as he learned that Jezebel, queen of Israel, wanted to kill him, what did he do? He didn't retreat to some Old Testament equivalent of a couch like I might've done and flip on the Disney Channel. He went "a day's journey into the wilderness and came and sat down under a broom tree. And he asked that he might die" (1 Kings 19:4).

He went to the desert.

When you read the Bible, it's amazing how often folks find themselves wandering in the desert or wilderness—places without much food or water, places of danger, and most especially, places of isolation. In the New Testament, the Greek word most often translated "wilderness" for our English-reading eyes is *erēmos* (or *erēmia*), which means "isolated place."[16] In the Bible, these isolated places are almost always locales for trial, of suffering, of tempering. No one has a particularly great time walking in the wilderness.

Depression is its own wilderness, the very definition of an isolated place. The solitude, separation, and loneliness can be profound.

But as isolated as it may be, the wilderness—be it physical, emotional, or spiritual—can be a place of encounter, too: encounter with God.

Moses had his chat with the burning bush in the wilderness. Then, when he led his people out of civilized Egypt, they all spent forty years out there, following pillars of cloud and fire, eating manna God dumped on the ground, receiving God's very own law. Prophets were perpetually running to the desert—either with the purpose of talking with God or just in a pique, like Elijah—finding that God had followed them out there. Many a Christian hermit and monk sought solitude with the Almighty in the most unpleasant of places. Pain, as much as we try to escape it or ease it, sometimes seems intrinsic to hearing God. To hear, as Elijah did, His "still, small voice."

It's a lovely phrase isn't it? That still, small voice. The translators for the King James Bible gave us that phrase, and many a translation still embraces it. But, according to Jewish scholars, that translation is not quite right. Rather, the Hebrew phrase *kol d'mamah dakkah* means "the sound of thin silence."[17] It's not the whisper we so often imagine. "It is probably a kind of silence that most of us have never experienced," reads a meditation from the Jerusalem Prayer Team. "Perhaps a total, complete silence."[18]

The closest I've come to such silence was in Canyonlands National Park in Utah, where a couple of friends and I went camping. At nearly 338,000 acres, Canyonlands is one of the country's biggest national parks and, when we went to visit it, one of the least visited. We went in early March—nighttime temperatures were still dipping below freezing—and one park ranger told us that there might be thirty to forty visitors in the entire place. It's the very definition of a biblical wilderness: It receives less than ten inches of precipitation a year, and anything that lives out there has to be tough. We went just a few months after my rodeo wipeout—when I was still rail-thin from my unintended diet and recovering from the depression's aftermath. I still wasn't sleeping well, and anyone who's been camping knows that it's not necessarily conducive to eight hours of shut-eye anyway. I was wide awake when the gray gloam of the morning began to bloom. I knew I wasn't going to sleep anymore, so I grabbed a stocking hat and crawled quietly out of the tent, past my snoozing friends, to watch the sunrise.

I sat on a rock and held my knees close to my neck, trying to keep warm as the sandstone rocks slowly changed from bands of gray to pink and red. Then, as the sun climbed behind me, it quietly painted the rock walls brilliant yellow. I felt it warm my back, saw as it painted me, too, splaying my shadow long and low on the ground—a lump of darkness blanketing a kaleidoscope of muted color.

And all was utterly quiet. The sound of a thin silence.

I mentioned earlier that I could count on one hand the times I felt God's presence fully, wholly, and powerfully with me. This was one of them. It cut through my cold, my lack of sleep, my stress, my sadness. I felt, that morning, whole. In the cup of God's hand.

I don't, as a rule, hear God talk to me. But in the silence that morning, I could feel Him breathe. And that is enough.

I wonder sometimes if depression can be more than a trial, more than a desert of isolation and despair. If we can force ourselves out of ourselves for a time, perhaps even this isolated place we walk through can be a place of encounter. Perhaps, in the static of our souls, we can still feel the thin silence of God.

We don't feel much like reading our Bibles or praying when we're depressed. But of all the onerous tasks that seem to loom over us in the throes of depression, these are perhaps less taxing than eating or taking a shower. And we may not feel God immediately in those times. Jesus spent forty days in the wilderness before Satan stopped pestering Him. Moses spent forty years. God's timetable is, unfortunately, not our own. It's possible we might not feel God at all.

Depression can make feeling anything pretty difficult.

But that doesn't mean He's not there. Sometimes, the silence isn't about God's absence, but His presence.

Why is one of the most powerful, most poignant, most mysterious three-letter words in the English language.

The only three-letter word that does *why* one better is this one: *God*.

My favorite Old Testament book is the book of Job. Its titular hero was certainly depressed, and he had all kinds of reason to be. He lost everything—his wealth, his family, his health. He sat in the ashes and scraped himself with a shard of pottery. And while many a preacher and Sunday school teacher said that Job never lost his trust in God through all his many ordeals, it strikes me that he got pretty angry with his circumstances all the same.

Job's experience with his friends might strike many Christians with depression as pretty familiar. He must have sinned to suffer so, they believe. And finally, by chapter 29, Job's patience is worn through. He tells them how righteous he's been and how grievously he's been treated in spite of it all. And he complains of the silence of God.

"I cry to you for help and you do not answer me," he says in Job 30:20. "I stand, and you only look at me."

Job cries out in the black silence he feels, demanding an answer. Why? Why make me suffer so? Why take away so much? Why have you forsaken me?

And then, a few chapters later, God speaks.

"Who is this who darkens counsel by words without knowledge?" God thunders in Job 38:2-3 (NKJV). "Now prepare yourself like a man; I will question you, and you shall answer Me."

And then God—in some of the most beautiful language put to pen—proceeds to give Job exactly zero answers.

It's gotta be the most powerful "because I said so" speech in world literature.

Why does God allow something as awful and seemingly without meaning as depression? Why does God allow His chosen people to suffer from it?

Maybe someday we'll know. Maybe someday God will tell us.

But He's not obligated. God is God.

So where does that leave us?

Let me leave the Bible for now and turn to another great saga with lots of men with beards—*The Lord of the Rings*.

As I suggested a few chapters ago, Frodo's burden—the bit of evil jewelry he carries—can look and feel a lot like depression in some ways. And Frodo must ask why at times too. Why is the ring so evil? Why wasn't it destroyed? And most especially, why did this burden fall on me? Like Job, he was just living his life, minding his own business.

In Peter Jackson's movie *The Lord of the Rings: The Fellowship of the Ring*, we find Frodo sitting around the mines of Moria, feeling sorry for himself.

"I wish the ring had never come to me," he tells Gandalf. "I wish none of this had happened."

Gandalf, the great wizard (whom the Catholic Tolkien said was somewhat analogous to an "angel" incarnate[19]), comforts Frodo by commiserating.

"So do all who live to see such times, but that is not for them to decide," Gandalf says. "All we have to decide is what to do with the time that is given to us."

Depression comes with no easy answers. The silence, at times, can be deafening. But in that silence, we can find beauty, too, and purpose. And instead of letting depression consume us, perhaps, with God's help, we can find the will to deal with it . . . and do some good in the world in spite of it.

PART II

UP

In which the author gets his act together,
starts running, and learns how better to alleviate
and manage depression, one boring act at a time.

CHAPTER 7

ONE FOOT IN FRONT
OF THE OTHER

*Courage is not having the strength to go on;
it is going on when you don't have the strength.*

THEODORE ROOSEVELT

IN THE MOVIE *CHARIOTS OF FIRE*, Scottish sprinter Eric Liddell
(played by Ian Charleson) tells his devout, disappointed sister,
Jenny, that he's going to race in the 1924 Olympics before heading
to China as a Christian missionary.

"I believe that God made me for a purpose," Eric tells Jenny.
"For China. But He also made me *fast*. And when I run, I feel His
pleasure."

When I run, I suppose I feel God's pleasure too: Him laughing
at me.

God made me for a purpose too. But He did not make me
fast. Or graceful. Or particularly coordinated. He did not give me
a love of running, or even an affinity for it.

But He did make me stubborn, and that's something. Because

even though it's a rare day I want to run, I still do it most days. It's a rare run that I enjoy, but I almost always enjoy having run.

And while it's perhaps a stretch to say that running saved my life, it is the single biggest cudgel that has kept my depression at bay for the last several years. I may not be fast, and honestly, I seem to be getting slower all the time. But I am sane, relatively speaking. And that's something.

My dislike of running came quite early in life. Like most kids, I enjoyed racing around the yard at first, particularly if I had fastened a pillowcase to my shoulders and could make it flap like a cape. But then came gym class, and by the second grade, I hated everything to do with gym on principle.

Our teacher was an ex-Army drill sergeant who had a face like a potato and always wore a stocking cap, making him look like a 1960s movie dockyard tough guy who, if you looked at him wrong, might whip out a crowbar and start thwacking you with it. He clearly knew the world was a hard and dangerous place filled with people who'd try to hurt you, and maybe kill you if they could. So why not teach by example? He wasn't teaching us second graders how to be healthier: It was like he was training a waist-high army for the inevitable commie invasion, and we had to be ready for anything.

We ran a lot. Boy, did we run. Up and down the gym, up and down the basketball court, up and down the Taos playground. Every time we finished up the latest death sprint, he'd ask us all if we felt like throwing up. If no one actually upchucked the peanut butter sandwich they had for lunch, our teacher would pronounce us "pretty much okay, fit-wise." I always felt like I was going to heave, but it was best to keep your head down and not make eye contact. If you did, he'd be liable to make you drop and give him twenty.

I avoided running after that. And by the time I got out of high school, I figured my running days were over. I got plenty of exercise through hiking and playing tennis and the occasional crazy game of putt-putt golf. That was enough. No one would ever make me run again.

But one of my best friends—Jeff Lamontagne—*did* run. He ran a marathon and a couple of half-marathons in college and, every few years, did a few more. He never claimed to be particularly fast either, but he kept preaching how much it helped him, both in body and mind. And remembering how messed up he was in seventh grade, I could see that maybe there's something to this running thing, after all.

Still, running seemed like the dumbest of all possible sports. No one kept score. In the sort of long-distance races that Jeff was doing, most people didn't even care about winning. What's the point of competing if you're not going to win?

"It's all about staying healthy and being active!" Jeff would say.

"Yeah, yeah," I'd say, likely taking another bite of my Quarter Pounder. *Whatever.*

But then I had my rodeo wipeout, and with it the willingness to change some patterns in my life.

Wendy and I had just helped Jeff and his wife, Suzanne, move. My old, old best friend, Bret,* the same guy who rescued me from the pea gravel in fourth grade, was there too. I was just a few weeks removed from my wipeout, I think, and neither my stomach nor my head were functioning just right. I loved everyone in

---

* He's nine months older than I am. And boy, does he look it.

that room, and I'd known Jeff and Bret for, roughly, ever. But the static was really humming that night. I felt pretty horrible about myself—that I was being both boring and foolish—and I wanted nothing more than to open up their apartment door, run down the stairs, and keep running until I either made it home or collapsed and died.

But some social niceties must be preserved, even amongst the best of friends. So instead of making a break for it, I excused myself to go to the bathroom (my tummy had already gotten a running start) to attend to business and see if I could whip my brain into some semblance of functionality. And after a few minutes in there, I heard Jeff ask Wendy, "Is he all right?"

"His stomach's still bothering him some," she said. It was my cue to return to the party. In a few more minutes.

By the time I got to the living room, Jeff was talking about running again in that friendly, proselytizing way of his. How *wonderful* it was. How *healthy* it was. How *fun* it was. We didn't have to run *marathons* necessarily, he told us. We could run just a teensy-weensy race—like the BOLDERBoulder. It's just ten kilometers, he said—a little over six miles. You don't even have to run the whole thing. And it's fun! People line the streets and cheer you on! Bands play on almost every block! You end in the University of Colorado's Folsom Field! It's an experience like no other.

Two things to know about Jeff: He's as persuasive as a good politician and as dogged as, well, a dog, I guess. He's talked all of his friends into doing some crazy things on occasion with this lethal blend of charisma and bullheadedness. Years earlier, he talked me into constructing an entire miniature golf course at my grandparents' cabin. In the dark. In the rain.

But he did make the BOLDERBoulder sound kinda fun. And six miles . . . well, I'd never run six miles before, but I thought it might be possible. I mean, I hiked that far, and farther, with some regularity. But I hate to run, and—

Then Bret turned to me.

"I'll do it if you do it," he said.

I don't know whether, while I was in the bathroom, my friends had conspired against me. But no matter: It worked. If Bret—whose last real exercise was summer-school bowling class—could pull himself away from work to train for a 10K, I could too. And who knows? It might do me good.

Training wasn't *fun*, exactly: I'd wake up an hour earlier than I was used to and run up and down the hills in my neighborhood, dodging cars and dogs and the occasional deer. But I admit that I started to enjoy seeing the sun rise, and after a few months, I felt "pretty much okay, fit-wise." And the race proved to be even better than advertised.

Colorado boasts few cities as picturesque as Boulder. We ran through beautiful neighborhoods filled with brick houses and irises, and cruised through its downtown corridor filled with folks cheering us on. Little kids would hold up signs encouraging mommy or daddy. Residents sometimes gave out free bacon or beer—standard running snacks, I was led to believe. And when I entered the stadium, a roar went up from the thousands in the bleachers. I chose to believe it was for me, not the band of Marines jogging in unison just a few yards in front of me.

Maybe running's not so bad, I thought.

And even when I found out otherwise, it was too late to stop. I've been running ever since. I don't think it's a coincidence that since I've started running, I've not had a true *lay-me-out, bury-me-now, flat-on-my-back* depressive episode. Like many people, I run to stay healthy . . . but for me, it's about my mental health as much as anything. While office-bound critics remind me that *The*

Complete Book of Running author James Fixx died at fifty-two and that my knees will surely shoot straight out of my skin one day, I know how I feel mentally if I don't run for several days. Trust me, it's not pretty.

You don't need to run to stave off depression, of course. Lots of forms of exercise will do—almost anything to get the heart pumping and the lungs working a little harder. So what works well to keeps depression at bay? The first and most obvious is . . .

GETTING THE BODY MOVING

I realize that for those dealing with a serious depressive episode, getting up and going for a jog (or a swim or even a walk) sounds about as possible as getting out of bed and joining the Minnesota Vikings. Depression can increase your pain receptors, mess with your eating habits, and completely obliterate healthy sleep patterns—all of which can make exercise all the less appealing. Every step can feel like an impossibility.

I've been there. During my rodeo wipeout, Wendy made me go for a walk one day. It was a beautiful day—perfect for walking—and I wanted to make her happy, so I tried. We made it past just three or four houses before I told her I couldn't walk anymore and went back home.

But if you *can* get out, research suggests that few things are better for you than a little physical exercise. Indeed, an overwhelming number of studies show that exercise doesn't just help treat the symptoms of depression pretty effectively, but it stays effective over long periods of time.[1] In fact, according to researchers at Harvard

Medical School, exercise has been proven to be just as effective as antidepressants for some people.[2]

"Motion is lotion," my friend Tim Sanford from the Focus on the Family counseling staff tells me. "Moving, even small shuffles across the room and back, is lotion to the body, the mind, and the soul."

The process begins with simple chemistry and biology that might help override some of the biochemical problems that cause or are exacerbated by depression. Certainly, lots of intense training can release endorphins that can make you feel good, leading to the famous "runner's high." You feel stronger, happier—euphoric, even—and you're more resistant to pain. German researchers, extrapolating from studies on mice, suggest that exercise might even tap into the brain's "endocannabinoid system," which is the same effect on your brain that people experience when using marijuana.[3] (Thus, presumably, the similarities between the words endocannabinoid and cannabis, I'd assume.) The runner's high, these German scientists suggest, is no exaggeration: Running can make you feel like you've smoked weed without the nasty smell, failed drug tests, and the desire to eat whole bags of Doritos.

But while I've felt the runner's high, I think, it's not that common or that pronounced. Also, I tend to be *running* when it hits, eliminating some of the charm. And, like marijuana, its effects tend to give you a false sense of reality. Hey, if the runner's high hits around mile eight, I may feel like I'm ready to run across the state, no problem—possibly singing all the way. By mile thirteen, I know better.

But there's another way that running helps, according to Harvard, and you don't need to run eight miles to find it.

Exercise—again, not just running, but swimming or walking or playing tennis or whatnot—fosters the release of proteins that make your nerve cells grow and connect with other nerve cells (according to Harvard).[4] That growth and interconnectivity apparently makes you just feel better and more balanced. Other studies have found that it smooths out our brains' responses to stress, tamps down on "excessive inflammation" (though the blisters I sometimes get might beg to differ) and helps other physiological friction points.[5]

And if you're exercising outside—especially in nature—the benefits become even more pronounced. One study found that participants who spent a couple of nights in the forest had lower levels of cortisol, a prominent stress-marker.[6] Several studies have found that time in nature can help combat depression, even major depression.[7] Stanford University reported another study that found folks who took a ninety-minute walk in the woods "showed decreased activity in a region of the brain associated with a key factor in depression."[8]

Then there's the obvious: When you're exercising, you likely just feel better about yourself. You feel healthier and more in control. You may feel like you look better. You likely have more energy, which allows you to do the things that you enjoy doing for longer.

Running is not a great tool to lose weight, oddly. But I know when I'm training for a marathon, I tend to lose anywhere from ten to fifteen pounds. Vain as this may sound, I feel different about myself when I weigh 165 pounds than when I weigh 180. When my clothes fit better, I feel better. And that's one less trigger for me that might send me down the *worthless* trajectory that seems so common in my depression.

CONNECTION

I was drawn to running, in part, because it was as solitary a sport as you can get. Being the introvert that I am, I try to avoid other people whenever possible. And honestly, I do enjoy running by myself. I don't need someone else to keep me entertained. Running by myself, the process of pounding the pavement, helps me work through the stress and challenges of the day, keeping me from falling into mental traps that are difficult to crawl out of. And that's great.

But I've noticed a disturbing tendency in me: The less I'm with people, the less I want to be with people. And the more isolated I am, the more my mind turns inward, fixating on stressors and problems and my own failures. And that's obviously not a particularly healthy place to be.

So I've discovered the pleasures, even the joys, of running with other people too. When I run with someone else, it forces my mind outward. I'm not just focused on moving forward—a good thing in itself—but moving forward *with* someone. The running becomes a relationship. It sounds cheesy, but there's something innately healthy about pushing away from the *me* and running toward the *us*.

Years after Jeff talked me into running the BOLDERBoulder, he talked me into running a marathon with him. (He just doesn't quit, that Jeff.) No longer was six miles enough: Now it was twenty-six. And when you're as slow as I am, training runs can last for two, three, even four hours. That's a long time to listen to your own feet strike dirt. Thankfully, Jeff made it easy on me: We did our long runs together—alternating between Denver and my home base in Colorado Springs.

Now, Jeff and I have been friends since seventh grade. We shared a lot of our childhoods together and became as close as two heterosexual guys can be. But when even the best of childhood friends become adults, there's a natural tendency to separate a bit. We each got married, had kids, worked demanding jobs. Those long weekend runs gave us a chance to reminisce about the old days and commiserate about the new ones—unpack family dramas and workplace frustrations and not just remember who we were, but also become more familiar with who we are. It allowed us to foster an entirely new aspect of our friendship. And that's pretty cool.

Running has also given me the chance to connect with my own kids—especially my daughter, Emily—in a really nifty way.

As I kept running, my kids started engaging in the sport too. We ran the BOLDERBoulder together for several years, sometimes bringing other friends or family members along for the run. In high school, both Colin and Emily started competing in cross-country. Sometimes, when I'd be training for a marathon, they'd be training for a half. And when Colin was out of the house and Emily was still in it, Em and I began to train for our respective races together. On long-run days, we'd start out and run, say, six or seven miles together—perfect for Emily's half-marathon training. Then Wendy would pick up Emily at a designated spot and I'd run another six or seven miles to prepare for my marathon.

And then, she decided to start running marathons with me. We weren't just running six miles together. We'd go for ten, fourteen, sometimes twenty-two miles. That's a lot of time to talk.

Those runs were, for me as a dad, remarkable. Both Emily and I are pretty private people. It's uncomfortable for either of us to open up too much in person.* But if I keep my soul in the psychic equivalent of a safe-deposit box, Em banks hers in a moated castle guarded by dragons. She doesn't talk much about her hopes or fears with Wendy and me. She doesn't like showing a lot of emotion. When she got married and I saw her in her wedding dress

---

* Writing, as you can tell, is a different story.

for the first time, I felt like I'd lost and gained the whole world at the same time. I teared up as if someone had literally stuffed onions in my eyes, and every sliver of onion was somehow playing *Old Yeller*. Emily treated the moment like she was opening a checking account.

She is, come to think of it, just as taciturn as I was for so many years with my parents. Curse heredity.

But during that first spat of training runs—and in all the many, many that followed—we talked. Not about big important issues, necessarily. We'd talk about books and movies, about vacations and gardening and relatives and, oddly, skin care products. One morning, we spent an entire two-and-a-half-hour training run discussing breakfast food.

That's the funny thing about real connection: You don't need to pour out your soul. You just need to share stuff—stuff you enjoy, stuff you hate, the stuff that makes your everyday life neat or irritating. While some would argue that meaningful connection means always talking about "meaningful" things, I think "meaningful" can be pretty relative.

You don't have to talk about your fear of death. You can talk about your fear of clowns. You don't have to talk about politics or philosophy or the important essences in life (though you can if you want to). You can talk about the merits (or lack thereof) of turkey bacon. It's still connection. And in some ways, those more superficial connection points can feel just as profound as—maybe even more than—those showy bits of soul you might regurgitate only to your priest or counselor.

And as we talked, we shared experiences that most dads never get to share with their daughters: Watching a coyote dart across the path. Listening to the ice sing on a frozen lake. Grossing out together over a really filthy portable toilet. We ran in twenty-degree weather and in eighty-degree weather, through forests and home-less encampments and, once, an unexpected turn-of-the-century-themed arts-and-crafts festival.

One morning, we ran eight miles in a bitter, driving wind that we weren't prepared for. We stopped in a grove of ponderosa pines, and I doled out our halfway-point snack (yep, we still had another eight to go)—fruit rolls that were stiff with cold. I still remember Em peeling off her mittens to stuff the roll into her mouth—a tiny, crystalized strip at a time—her nose blue, her feet shaking in her running shoes. We were both pretty miserable. But turns out, misery really does love company. Sometimes our most uncomfort-able moments become the fodder for shared stories later. They stop being moments you'd rather forget and become moments you love to remember. They become, in short, *adventures*. As an introvert, I sometimes forget that. Running with someone—with Emily, mostly—helps me remember.

But even when I'm not running with someone, I still feel that connection—that link to a broader world. You're in that world. You feel, on some level, an intimate part of it, even if you're just running by. The trees and grasses that line the trail, or the houses and businesses you pound past on the sidewalk, feel more a part of you than when you're just driving by them. In a car, you feel inher-ently an interloper in the life buzzing all around you—an isolated missile zipping past. When you walk or run, you're a participant in that life. You're a piece of all around you, an intricate part of God's creation.

I believe that separation—the divorce we sometimes feel from each other, from the world around us, even from God—can be a critical element of depression. Sometimes, exercise can help, if not completely heal, the divisions we feel. To patch them and knit them closer together.

CONSTANCY

I was never one for order. In high school, my bedroom floor had a nice mulch of old homework papers. My locker looked like the lair of a Dark Age monster. I was kinda proud of how chaotic my world looked to the outside, because order was antithetical to who I was and who I wanted to be. I imagined myself a poet, after all. I would let the art and spirit take me where it would. I thought that, like so many of the great artists and writers and dreamers I admired, I'd experience the world like a leaf on the wind, going where it blew and landing where it wished. I might isolate myself like van Gogh, or travel the world like Hemingway, or live a life of uncompromising chaos like, oh, the Rolling Stones. Whatever it looked like, my life would serve the art I felt inside me, the stories I longed to tell. I would feel every emotion deeply—the happiness, the sadness, the hope, the despair. Because that's what poets do, right?

Of course, van Gogh cut off his ear, Hemingway wound up shooting himself, and clearly, Keith Richards has made some pact with the devil, because nothing else really explains how the dude could still be alive in 2019.

Turns out, there's something to this whole "order" thing after all.

Disorder gets me down. I think it always did. Now, I'm no neat freak: I let papers pile up in my office more than I should, and Wendy wonders why I never rinse off my plates. But if things get too bad, I find the need to restore order to my little self-created environment: I feel better when there's structure I can lean on. And if I have a solid sense of structure and organization underneath the mess, it allows me to deal with the disorder overlaying it all a bit more productively.

In my life, running serves as that underlying structure. Like the baseline of a piece of jazz music or the two-by-fours lurking under the drywall, running undergirds and, in some ways, supports everything else I do.

It works like this: Say I'm training for a marathon. I know that, to run the marathon's 26.2 miles, I'll need to put in about seven to nine months worth of serious, structured running: five runs every week, if I can manage—four "short" runs and one long run every weekend. Sometimes I think I should do more, and admittedly I sometimes do a little less on a given week. But that's the baseline for me. If I do *much* less, I'll likely fail in my ultimate goal of finishing the marathon. You can fake a lot of things, but if you fake your marathon training, the marathon will know.

And thus every other aspect of my life—even though those other aspects are, technically, more important than a little marathon—revolves around those training runs. They become the underlying framework for my life, the shelves for my life's books, the Christmas tree for my life's ornaments. Everything else needs to fit itself around those runs, and even my inherent laziness takes a back seat to them. *Want to take the night off and watch a terrible movie on Netflix?* Nope, sorry, gotta get my mileage in. *Want to mope around and eat Cheetos?* Sure, but after my run. *How about sleeping in on Saturday?* Can't. I'm meeting Emily at 7:30 for an eight-miler.

Training requires a certain level of accountability, which I think can be in itself a strong guard against some forms of depression. (More on that in the next chapter.) But it's all about being accountable to yourself. And honestly, that sense of personal accountability is something I both desperately need and am really poor at giving myself absent a reason for it. Absent my running.

I'm an example of that even now. Even as I extol the praises of running, I've not run for a week now. I have nothing to train for, and so those other areas of my life start to encroach. I've got movies to see. Deadlines to meet. A stupid book on depression to write. *I'm so busy,* I tell myself. *Too busy to run today. Maybe tomorrow.* But tomorrow comes and the busyness isn't any better. It grows harder and harder to make myself go out and run. I can feel my tummy push harder against my jeans. My brain feels a little more disjointed, a little more filled with the static of my depression. My whole being feels like your mouth does when you wake up in the morning, in need of a good brush and gargle.

It's time to sign up for another race. Because having a goal to literally run toward is the best way I know to force myself to run. Because even though I spend so many extra hours running—hours I really can't afford to spend—I know that if I don't, my depressive tendencies have another avenue to claim more control over my life. The whispers of worthlessness might grow louder. My sleep will get worse. The clutter of my life will go from inconveniently messy to inexcusably dirty, requiring that much more labor-intensive scrubbing later on.

Ironically, running itself can become an analogy for depression.

It was a beautiful day, except for the pain.

You could smell the sea air, hear the waves lap against the boats we were running beside. But I barely noticed. Emily and I were just a quarter mile into the Newport Marathon in Newport, Oregon, when I felt the first real twinge in my back.

I was not surprised. I figured it would come, but I hoped it'd be later.

Marathons are *hard*: hard to run them and hard to train for them. I've been pretty lucky in my running career to stay clear of injuries. And sometimes, even when Emily and I had some injurious setbacks, we were able to—perhaps miraculously—pull through. When Emily ran her first marathon, she forgot her shoes at home. She ran the whole thing in a borrowed pair of running shoes and earned a trophy for her age group. In her third marathon, she'd struggled with knee problems during our entire training regimen. Next time we went into training, she developed some persistent soreness in her knee. It was hurting so bad toward the end of our training that she sometimes looked like an especially skinny and fleet Quasimodo—limp-galloping toward the parking lot. When it came time for our race at Disney World, she brought a knee brace and scads of ibuprofen. But even though Em hadn't had a pain-free, limp-free run in months, she ran the marathon just fine. It was, in fact, her fastest time ever. It was a little racing miracle.

But during *this* marathon, when I could've used a miracle myself, I wasn't so blessed. Six weeks before the Newport Marathon, during a long training run, I'd pulled something in my back. It's the sort of injury I probably should've anticipated. When you reach a certain age, your muscles and bones get a little sick of being with you all these years, and they eventually take it out on you. And honestly, it didn't feel that bad at first. And with our marathon so near, I figured I'd just keep training and gut it out.

That hadn't worked.

So I figured I'd rest it for a week and hope not to lose too much muscle.

That hadn't worked, either.

Part of me (a small part) thought about skipping the marathon. But Emily and I had trained so long and so hard, and I felt like I would be letting her down. Plus, Newport's medals are really cool—not metal medals, but glass ones, each one a unique creation from one of the local glass shops. I really wanted that medal if I could figure out a way to make it to the finish line.

A quarter mile in, I started to hurt. After two miles, I was pretty sure I'd have to drop out somewhere along the way.

But the medal. I thought. *But Emily.*

The pain didn't stop. But remarkably, it stopped getting worse for a while. I found that if I turned my right foot just so and worked my left leg a little harder, I could limp along at a pretty healthy pace. I hurt, but some level of discomfort is *sometimes* part of the territory even on *good* long runs. If I could just keep pushing forward, maybe my aching back would loosen up.

But when you try to protect one set of muscles by overtaxing another, it opens your body to all sorts of chaos.

Same thing is true in depression, too, by the way. You can try to ignore your pain, or minimize it by concentrating on other things, or push yourself more and more, hoping that the pain will go away. And sometimes, that'll work for a bit. But to ignore or avoid or minimize what's really going on will eventually catch up with you. Your depression will rise up like the Creature from the Black Lagoon and wrap you in its arms. And then, there's no pretending that everything's all right. There's no chance to cowboy up. You acknowledge that something's going on and accept that you're going to need to deal with it—no matter what plans you had for the day or week or year.

Halfway through, my plans for this marathon had been utterly obliterated. My back was feeling better, but only because so many other areas of my body were hurting so much worse. Even as the clouds slowly burned away into blue, even with birds and flowers and water at every turn, the course had long lost its beauty. Every step hurt in a dozen places. Every effort I made to talk felt false and strained.

I can't keep going, I thought. *There's no way I can keep this up for another thirteen miles. No. Possible. Way.*

But if I've learned anything from marathons, it's this: When you feel you can't go on, you can.

You can.

The human body can run 26.2 miles. But it doesn't particularly like to.

Sure, we're built for distance. Deer and cheetahs can embarrass us in sprints, but pile on the mileage and we begin to catch up. Some experts say that, on a hot enough day, a man—a fast man, admittedly—can beat a horse in a full marathon. But covering that sort of ground comes with a cost. No matter how diligently we train, no matter how many carbohydrates we load up on the night before, and no matter how many snacks we bring to eat along the way, most of us run out of fuel. Around mile twenty or so, all the carbs in our system are gone.[9] Our bodies can't process the simple sugars we're consuming during the run quickly enough. So our system starts poking around for something else to eat: fat and muscle, primarily. And while burning fat is one of the reasons we runners run, burning muscle is something else entirely. It's a little like if your car ran out of gas and started gobbling up your carburetor.

They call this "hitting the wall." The dizziness hits. The nausea. Some people get headaches. For me, it's as if my body just announced, "Yep, we're done. Sorry 'bout that." The run turns into a shuffle, if we're able to run at all. We cruise through the first twenty miles, no problem. And then, suddenly, we're coldcocked by our own mortality.

I've heard some runners call the last six miles of a marathon the race's "second half," and that feels about right. The race switches from a physical challenge to a mental one. The body's done: It's up to the mind to push you through to the end.

I've read strategies to avoid the wall, but I've rarely managed it. By mile twenty-two, most every part of my body hurts, even my teeth.

But that's not the worst of it: Pain's just part of what you sign up for when you're marathoning. What you don't expect—and it surprises me every time—is that sense of *quit* in the body. You know there's a finish line up there somewhere. But some terrible part of your brain tells you that the race will never end. We've been taught that we can meet any challenge if we just put our mind to it—that we can do amazing things if we just believe we can. The wall is when our body tells us, "Wanna bet?" Every physical synapse reaching your brain says, "Enough. Stop already."

And sometimes, for our own health, we must listen. Your heart isn't pumping right. Your knee stops bending as it should. Most marathoners have quit a race at some point. And if I keep doing marathons, I probably will someday too.

But I haven't yet.

When I feel like I can't go on, I do anyway. When almost everything inside of me says *stop*, a small voice keeps telling me to go. Slowly, maybe. But go. *I can take another step*, it says. *I can make it to the next tree.* The race is no longer twenty-six miles, but a series of tiny, painful, reachable goals. Covering another four miles feels impossible when you hit the wall. But getting to the top of the hill? *Yeah, I can do that.*

And so the miles wear away, yard by yard. I feel a little like a kid whose parents are forcing him to eat his peas: one more bite, one less pea. Each step is a step I'm done with, a step I don't have to take anymore.

Anne Lamott took the title of her book *Bird by Bird* from a nearly failed research project. Her ten-year-old brother had procrastinated writing a huge school report involving scads of birds. Suddenly, it was the day before the report was due, and as he sat surrounded by research books, he was close to tears, paralyzed by the immensity of the task. Lamott writes: "Then my father sat down beside him, put his arm around my brother's shoulder, and said, 'Bird by bird, buddy. Just take it bird by bird.'"[10]

That's the secret to marathoning. That's, I think, the secret to life—especially a life riven by anxiety and depression. Take it bird by bird.

Bird by bird. Breath by breath. Step by step. So goes the end of every marathon. And then, somehow—nearly miraculously—I find myself on the other side of the wall, as if through sheer force of will I dematerialized it and shuffled right through to the other end. I'm still tired. I'm still in pain. But I know—*know*—that I can make it. Sometimes it's with a mile and a half yet to go. Sometimes, it's almost within sight of the finish line. But I'm sure I will get there.

And that is like no other feeling I've ever felt. It's not glee or exultation or happiness or even simple relief, but a hard-earned sense of joy.

And so it is with depression.

When you're in the throes of depression, life itself can feel like an agony. It seems to sap everything you need to keep going: your desires, your interests, your relationships. Like mile twenty-three, everything looks curiously flat, everything feels dull. The pain never leaves. And here's the thing: Sometimes, you can feel like it'll never end. That you'll be on this horrific slog forever. And sometimes the pain, or the weariness, or the seeming endlessness of it all makes us want to quit. We despair and stop moving. Some stop moving forever.

So what must we do? *Just. Keep. Moving.* Maybe we can't imagine facing another day. But let's crawl through the next hour, and then the next. Maybe we can't fathom stepping outside the house. But getting out of bed? Taking a shower? Maybe we can do that, and we'll worry about the next small goal after that.

Because here's the truth: We've got a medal waiting for us. As hard as things may be, as hopeless as we might feel, there is hope. Depression can be quelled (if not always completely conquered). Depressive episodes eventually lose their grip with effort and treatment. Those who struggle with more chronic depression can find tools to keep it in check and ward off the worst of it. Exercise is just one of them. Life can do more than go on and on. It can be filled with beauty and joy and achievement and love.

But to reach that point, you gotta break through the wall. And to break through, you have to keep moving.

I pressed on in Newport, but with some adjustments—and a little encouragement from my running partner.

"My back . . ." I started to say. "Em, I—"

"Need to walk?" Emily said. "Thank goodness! I'm *exhausted*!"

And so we walked for a while. Then we ran as far as I could, and then walked some more. I don't know if Emily really was grateful to take it as slowly as I needed to, but no matter: She stuck with me anyway. We watched runners seemingly sprint past us as we talked. We pointed out the flowers we saw, strange to our Colorado eyes. We watched the seagulls float over the Yaquina River, the wide waterway we ran beside. I kept telling Em she could run ahead if she wanted: She could finish the thing an hour before me, if she wanted. But instead, she told me that this was one of the most enjoyable marathons we'd ever done together. And whether it was a lie or not, I was glad to have her with me.

We didn't set any personal records in Newport. By mile twenty-four, we weren't even running at all. If I tried, my legs would cramp something awful. So we walked along Yaquina Bay as other marathoners shuffled by us, their footfalls adding a backdrop to our conversation.

Then, with twenty-six miles in the books and just the point-two to go, I tried to run again. And improbably, everything worked. Emily thought that running the last two-tenths of a mile after walking the last three was just plain crazy, given how nice a time we were having. But I started the marathon running, and I wanted to finish it running. So we ran down the hill, past a worried Wendy (who expected to see us forty minutes earlier) and her iPhone camera. We even mustered a smile. In the picture it doesn't look like we're moving at all, but we are. We're just slow, that's all. When your knees don't bend and your back doesn't twist and you don't have enough strength to lift your feet higher than a couple of inches, that's the way you look.

We crossed the finish line, collected our medals, and staggered off for a free bagel or two. And then we sat down, put our swelling feet up and rested: Not by the side of the road, as I so much wanted to do miles—ages—ago. Not in defeat, not in submission to the pain. We rested in victory. No matter that hundreds of runners finished before we did. We finished. And in so doing, we won.

Around AD 54, in his first letter to the Corinthians, Paul wrote about running the race so that you will win the prize.

It took him another ten to twelve years to write about running again, this time to his friend Timothy. He was in a Roman prison cell then, waiting for his own execution. By then, he'd been abandoned by many. He'd suffered deeply. "I am already being poured out as a drink offering, and the time of my departure has come."

And then he added this famous phrase: "I have fought the good fight, I have finished the race, I have kept the faith" (2 Timothy 4:6-7).

You don't need to win to win. You do, however, need to finish. It's not easy. It's not easy for any of us whether we suffer from depression or not. Life is hard. Life can wring you out like a washcloth, and sometimes the pain and grief and hardships we experience along the way can feel like too much to bear. It's so easy to check out in one way or another. To give up.

But to finish the race—to stare down our setbacks and suffering, to push through the wall and push away our despair—this is the stuff of victory. To persevere despite our despair and find our place in God's plan—this is the stuff of heroism. God knows who we are and where we are, and He asks us to move forward anyway. We must fight the fight. We must run the race. We must find the finish and claim our medals and then—only then—we rest. And we shall feel God's pleasure.

CHAPTER 8

A TIME FOR EVERYTHING

It's not about you.

THE ANCIENT ONE, *Doctor Strange*

ON FEBRUARY 5, 1865, Abraham Lincoln sat for what would be his last formal photograph. He'd been reelected by then, and the Civil War was drawing to a close. And perhaps that's why, in the very last image taken of him that Sunday—one that was initially thrown out because the glass negative was cracked—the president seems to smile.

It's strange to see his mild, Mona Lisa grin. People rarely smiled for photos back in those early days: The time needed to hold a pose and for long exposures prevented a lot of levity. But when we take a closer look at Lincoln's face, we see something else remarkable. Bags rest under his sunken eyes, his face is lined with well-earned wrinkles. It's a sad, careworn face, and the smile adorns it like a crocus emerging from a blanket of snow.

Read much about Lincoln, and you'll find that both the smile and the sadness were integral parts of his character. He loved a good laugh, and he appreciated funny stories—especially the ones he told. But he struck many as painfully morose, too. "He was a sad-looking man," wrote Lincoln's law partner William Herndon. "His melancholy dripped from him as he walked."[1] Artist Francis B. Carpenter said that Lincoln's was "the saddest face I ever attempted to paint."[2]

They called him Honest Abe. And his face doesn't lie.

For years, especially in his early years, Lincoln dealt with what was known then as hypochondriasis—not hypochondria as we understand it, but some sort of ailment of the abdomen where, according to Lincoln biographer Doris Kearns Goodwin, the source of our emotions was thought to lay.[3] Now, we'd almost certainly identify Lincoln's early melancholy as depression. He confessed to friends that he often thought about suicide.[4] Robert Wilson said of Lincoln, "Although he appeared to enjoy life rapturously, still he was the victim of terrible melancholy. He sought company, and indulged in fun and hilarity without restraint . . . [but] when by himself, he told me that he was so overcome with mental depression, that he never dare carry a knife in his pocket."[5]

He was perhaps at his most sorrowful in the winter of 1840 and '41. In her book *Team of Rivals: The Political Genius of Abraham Lincoln*, Goodwin writes that Lincoln spent weeks in "mourning" after he broke up with Mary Todd (whom he later married) and grieving over the expected departure of his friend Joshua Speed.[6] He stopped going to the Illinois General Assembly (for which he was serving a fourth term). He withdrew from social activities. In a letter to his friend John Stewart in 1841, Lincoln wrote, "I am now the most miserable man living. If what I feel were equally distributed to the whole human family, there would not be one cheerful face on the earth. Whether I shall ever be better I cannot tell; I awfully forebode I shall not. To remain as I am is impossible; I must die or be better, it appears to me."[7]

Eventually, Lincoln found a way out of his malaise. And he did it by getting and staying busy. As Goodwin writes, "He understood . . . that in times of anxiety it is critical to 'avoid being idle,' that 'business and conversation of friends' were necessary to give the mind 'rest from that intensity of thought, which will some times wear the sweetest idea threadbare and turn it to the bitterness of death.'"[8]

I hear that Mr. Lincoln made something of himself a few years later.

"A tendency to melancholy," Lincoln said, "is a misfortune, not a fault."[9]

As we've seen, plenty of people suffer from that tendency. Depression is the leading cause of disability in the world, according to the Anxiety and Depression Association of America.[10] The World Health Organization estimates that depression accounts for $1 trillion in lost productivity worldwide.[11]

But look at history, and you'll see scads of depressed people (as near as we can figure, anyway) who overcame their depression, or managed it enough, to make massive contributions to the world.

Many biographers believe that Lincoln's two most successful generals, Ulysses S. Grant and William Tecumseh Sherman, also suffered from depression. Grant was pretty much drummed out of the army in 1854 because of his depression (or, more accurately, the drinking triggered by his depression).[12] At the outset of the Civil War, Sherman declared that the Union would need 250,000 men to quell the rebellion; when the media called him mad,* and suffering

---

* In truth, Sherman had underestimated about fourfold.

from the strain of his military duties, he resigned, returned home to Ohio, and spent his time there contemplating suicide.[13] Both successfully navigated their mental issues—Sherman through the support of his family and Grant with getting back to work—to help lead the Union army to victory. "[Grant] stood by me when I was crazy, and I stood by him when he was drunk," Sherman said. "And now, sir, we stand by each other always."[14]

Many believe that Winston Churchill dealt with depression, too, calling it a "black dog."[15] (Others, though, say he was just moody.)[16] Martin Luther King Jr. suffered from severe depression. He attempted suicide when he was a boy,[17] and apparently his own staff tried to get him into psychiatric treatment late in his life.[18] Mahatma Gandhi openly spoke of his struggles with depression throughout his career.[19] Leadership and depression are so often connected that Dr. Nassir Ghaemi decided it was no coincidence. He wrote *A First-Rate Madness: Uncovering the Links Between Leadership and Mental Illness*. He believes there might be some benefits to being a bit off your emotional rocker. The humility that comes with depression, for instance, may help good leaders stay grounded, where "normal" folks in leadership positions let all that power go to their heads. "People like Lincoln don't overestimate themselves, even though they have a great deal of power," he told *Merion West*.[20]

But for any of those alleged benefits to come into play, the depressed person has to first pull himself or herself out of bed.

That's not easy when you're depressed. And if you are depressed, you may read what follows and think, "Don't be daft, man! I don't want to do *anything*, much less take on duties and responsibilities, which cause stress, which put me here in the first place!"

First, kudos to you for using the word "daft," which isn't used enough in my opinion. Secondly, I hear you. Check back in chapter 5, and you'll see that workplace stress was a pretty big component for my own wipeout.

But life is full of paradoxes, and this is one of them: When you've been knocked down, the very elements that might've put your keister on the carpet are the very same elements that can help you get up again. You just might need to modify them a little.

If, as I said, exercise helps lay down a jazz baseline for me living a rewarding life and coping with depression, the following serves as the rest of the tune. These particular tools and instruments might not work for you, so keep that in mind . . . but they do for me. As I move through each day, I try to keep the music going. And that means . . .

STAY IN RHYTHM

Almost all music, even freeform jazz, lives within a certain structure: Songs are separated into measures, and how "long" those measures (or bars) are is determined by the song's time signature. If you see a piece of sheet music that reads "4/4" at the front (one number "4" on top of another), that means four quarter notes (or two half notes or sixteen sixteenth notes, you get the picture) can fit in a measure. A piece of music under a 3/4 time signature will only contain three quarter notes per bar, etc.

Now, within this structure musicians toss in tons of variety, not just in the actual notes hit, but how long those notes last. They might be quarter notes, but no one's telling you how long those quarter notes actually have to *last*. You can hold a quarter note till February if you want. You can even speed up or slow down the pace in the middle of the song. But the structure—the measures and the time signatures—ensures that the song won't simply descend into chaos. It keeps the song in rhythm.

For me, routine helps give my days rhythm. I like to wake up around the same time on weekdays. I like to read the newspaper while eating breakfast (which I realize makes me sound like some sort of holdover from the 1950s, but there it is). I tend to do my get-ready things in the same order every day, and usually at the same time if I can. That seventy-five-minute routine I follow before work helps me dive into my relatively unstructured, unpredictable workday feeling grounded and capably adjustable.

This routine doesn't happen all the time. Some weeks, this routine doesn't happen at all. But when it does, I feel just a wee bit more at peace for the rest of the day.

Admittedly, I'm boring. I don't pretend otherwise. There are those who despise routine, who consciously scrap patterns and regimens if they feel too overly tied down by them. For them, *routine* means *rut*. But for me, routine isn't so much a rut in the road as it is a guardrail—something that keeps me from careening off some huge cliff, like Toonces the Driving Cat.*

Not that I'll go off all at once. But I know that when the paper doesn't show up on time, or I have to skip breakfast to record a podcast, I feel "off." And the more mornings I'm off, the crankier I become.

I'm not alone in this. Those routine-haters aside, I think most of us tend to find comfort in routine, even if we don't know it. Only then we don't call it routine: We call it *tradition*. That's one of the reasons why lots of church services tend to follow a certain predictable cadence: They're comforting. Many holidays have the same sort of charm. Families can follow the same general "schedule" over Christmas Eve and Christmas Day for decades, even through generations. (My own family, without fail, eats lasagna

---

* You don't know who Toonces the Driving Cat is? Search for it on YouTube. Don't worry. I'll wait.

for Christmas Eve dinner, because that's what my mom did, and that's what *her* mom did.) Even opening the doors or checking off the boxes on the advent calendar can become a beloved, blessed tradition.

Fred Rogers, the iconic creator and star of *Mister Rogers' Neighborhood*, knew how important routine was to his young viewers. That's why every day he walked into his television house, he did exactly the same thing: Put on the sweater. Put on the sneakers. Sing "It's a Beautiful Day in the Neighborhood" in time with his start-of-the-show cadence. This routine wasn't completely static: Sometimes he'd toss a shoe in the air (which I loved). Sometimes his sweater zipper would get stuck (which made me nervous). But the rhythm was the same. Kids *needed* that rhythm. Most adults, I believe, do too—even if that rhythm's increasingly hard to come by. And when I talked with Fred Rogers's wife, Joanne, several years after he died, I got the feeling that Fred himself had a hankering for routine.

"He loved his swims in the morning," she told me. "That was one thing, I think, in his chemistry . . . he would get really cranky when he had to miss a swim."

I hear ya, Mister Rogers. I hear ya.

This doesn't mean we need to be slavish to routine. Unpredictability is a part of life. It always has been, and it's particularly true now. And change is quite often a good thing. I love to travel, in part, because it upends every routine in the books. But if change *is* the routine, or if the change is inherently stressful, we can be thrown off our game. When I give even my most unpredictable days a small window of normalcy, it makes me feel more in control (at least during that small window), and thus more able to deal with all the wild chaos that might be on the horizon.

LOOK OUT, NOT IN

If there's such a thing as a cheat code for getting past depression, it might be summarized in those four words: "Look out, not in." But they're a really tricky four words to internalize.

When we're depressed, we tend to turn inward. I do, anyway. It's all about *me*: what I think, how I feel, how miserable I am. And that pushes us into a sort of self-made prison. We're trapped in our own psyche, with only a tiny, high window to the outside world that we can't even reach.

Funny thing is, though, the door's unlocked. It might be heavy or squeaky or even stuck, but it is unlocked. And often, in depression, the real challenge is to simply find a way to walk to that door that traps us inside of ourselves and try the handle.

You'd think that, for all that depression takes away, it would give you at least this: humility. So many of us feel so worthless when we're in the grips of it, so out of step with those around us, that at least we would feel deeply what Paul wrote about in Ephesians 3:8, being "the very least of all the saints." But the self-denigration that often comes with depression isn't humility; it's pride. We think far more about ourselves and our own miseries than those around us. "Humility," wrote Peter Kreeft in his book *Back to Virtue*, "is thinking less *about* yourself, not thinking less *of* yourself."[21]

When I was suffering from my wipeout, Wendy had the right idea: get me out. Outside. Out of the basement. Out of myself. It took me some time to find the will and see the sense of it, but eventually I did. We've already covered the benefits of physically getting out and active. Mentally, though, we get out in two basic and overlapping ways: responsibilities and relationship.

During my first depressive episode, when I was in college, the thing that pulled me outside that depressive prison was . . . well, both. Colin's impending arrival was both a responsibility and a relationship, wrapped up in the guise of fatherhood. I had a little future someone who was going to need me. And Wendy, she needed me too. She's a strong woman, but she wasn't going to be able to do it alone. Instead of focusing on my own neuroses, I was forced to pay attention to someone else.

That focus didn't magically cure me, of course. Depression rarely if ever vanishes like Tinker Bell, with a wave of a wand and a shower of sparkles. In some ways, I felt more insecure than ever in the months and years after.

But when Wendy and Colin and I were just starting out, I didn't have time to dwell on all that insecurity. I had a job to do—quite literally. I got a job working for an upstart weekly paper in the mountain community of Woodland Park called the *High Mountain Sun*, and that required anywhere from sixty to seventy hours a week of my time. I covered everything for the paper, from city council meetings to high school sports. I took photos and helped design and lay out the newspaper too. When I covered a traffic accident or a drowning, I was reminded what real tragedy and despair looked like.

And when I came home, that home wrapped itself around me. Wendy and I might eat dinner on our threadbare couch while watching an old movie on our twelve-inch television. We might watch Colin play with laundry (one of his favorite things to do) or race around the coffee table, laughing hysterically as his diaper made that plastic squeak they do. Wendy and I slept on the floor in those days—we didn't have money for a bed—and even as I kept one ear open for mice scurrying around our dark, cheap apartment, I slept pretty soundly. I had way more worries than I had before or after, when my depression got the best of me. But those very worries, I think, ironically helped keep any depression at bay. I just didn't sit still long enough for the disease to sink its claws into me.

And even today, that pattern still holds true.

When depression threatens to grab me and pull me into a pit, work and relationships help me walk past. I don't think this is a denial or an avoidance technique as much as it is the therapeutic value of handling the day-to-day challenges in our lives—the equivalent of enjoying a good book so much you forget the time, or enjoying a good talk over coffee so much that your coffee gets cold. Yes, work becomes a distraction, and admittedly it can become an unhealthy distraction. But it doesn't need to be so. Sure, to wrap yourself in sorrow and anguish can feel good and right in the moment, and it can be important, too. Therapeutic. Sometimes that happens to me. I might start crying after an unexpected song pops up on my playlist or just press my head into my hands for a while, unable to do anything else. And to sink into myself for a moment and feel deeply, even if it means to feel miserable, can feel like a needle to a blister, a healthy relief to the system. But worrying over that blister, rubbing the wound as I tend to do, is not healthy. I need to have something to help me forget and move on. The work that I do can be deeply engaging, and I feel like I'm pretty good at it—and that, too, can help alleviate some of the worthlessness that my depression tends to bring to the party. When my depression tells me that I'm a terrible human being, I can say, "Well, at least I know how to use *diaphanous* in a sentence." And that's something.

Relationships can be even more valuable in helping to keep depression at bay. When you think that you're the most miserable person in the world, talking with friends and family helps keep you grounded and focused on other people—like, I think, God wants us to be. And they can help us remember that everyone has problems. And sometimes, the problems we have can help, directly or indirectly, our friends and the relationships they enjoy. "Bear one another's burdens, and so fulfill the law of Christ," Paul tells us in Galatians 6:2. We depressive types don't get diplomatic immunity from that law, and we might find that we enjoy observing it.

The responsibilities we take—for work, for home, for one another—can help us deal. And while those of us managing depression shouldn't take on more than we can realistically tackle (those same responsibilities can overwhelm us, too, triggering anxiety and stress), we shouldn't avoid responsibilities altogether because we're worried that any responsibility will be bad. Life is, after all, about taking on responsibility. It's about sharing those burdens.

Apply for a job you can do and think you'll like. Volunteer for a charity that you believe in. Do the dishes. Read a bedtime story. Take a long walk with a friend or family member. Help someone move. You get the idea. These can be very meaningful to the people you're helping—and meaningful to you, too. Get out and get involved. Again, I recall what Tim Sanford told me: *Motion is lotion*. Keep moving in body, mind, and spirit.

LOOK FORWARD, NOT BACK

"Do not be anxious about tomorrow," Jesus says, "for tomorrow will be anxious for itself" (Matthew 6:34).

That could've been written by a twenty-first-century mental health guru. It's still good advice—and maybe more important today than it was when Jesus first said it. Tomorrow is full of scary unknowns, and for folks who deal with anxiety issues, the future is often the last thing they should mull over if they want to lower their blood pressure and stay reasonably sane. I've spent most of my adult life dealing with deadlines, so I know how stressful *looking forward* can be.

But we're concentrating on depression here, not anxiety, and for me, many depressive triggers are rooted in the past ("Man, what a jerk I was twenty years ago") and the present ("Haven't changed much, have I?"). And while one of the characteristics of the affliction is its ability to rob you of your hope for the future, I find that the promise of tomorrow can encourage me today.

That promise can take the form of little things to look forward to—like the streetlights or signposts I'd try to reach while running the last part of a marathon. Years ago, when I felt my mental equilibrium just begin to slide into dangerous despair, I'd distract myself by thinking about a metaphorical carrot that might be dangling on my personal horizon. "I gotta stick around to see that new Marvel movie," I might think to myself. Or "Hey, the Denver Broncos could have a pretty good season next year. I'd like to see how that Von Miller guy does." The promise of these carrots was perhaps not dramatic in terms of my overall mental health: It wasn't as though I was looking from a twenty-story window and contemplating a jump before I thought of a potential Colorado Rockies run to the World Series. It's not like I could ever stand up in front of a crowd and say tearfully, "*Iron Man* saved my life." But when a negative thought started flitting across my mind like a blown leaf—*What have you got to look forward to, Paul?*—I could say, *The Broncos have the sixth pick in the draft, buddy. I've got plenty to look forward to.* String a few of these together, and I was ready to move past those depressive whispers and on to the rest of my life.

It's not just sports and entertainment that I use as mile markers on my mental health run, of course. Wendy and I love to travel. Moreover, I love to *plan* to travel, and I'm almost always working on a trip in the back of my mind (or at the front of my computer screen). I enjoy home improvement jobs: Few things jazz me more than the prospect of planting a few trees or slapping up a new light fixture or, heck, even redesigning a whole room. I've sometimes thought about moving just so Wendy and I would have another unfinished basement to keep us busy. And then, of course, there are the more traditional and important life-markers: birthdays and anniversaries, graduations and the possibility of grandkids and all the people we'd never want to leave behind.

This is where *looking forward* braids with *looking outward.* *Future* often holds hands with our hopes and expectations for friends and family. To watch your children grow can be a powerful carrot. To spend as much time as possible with your loved ones can be an incredible motivator. Maybe that's why when something goes wrong in the family—when a marriage falls apart or a child tells you she hates you or when you otherwise lose someone you love—it can feel even more devastating than it otherwise would. You're not just losing a person, you're losing all those future moments you hoped to spend with him or her. It not only crushes your today, it also robs your tomorrow.

But even the day-to-day grind can give you a little reason to get up in the morning: Those same deadlines that can stress me out are the same deadlines that pull me into the shower and push me to my desk—upright and awake and, most mornings, at least semi-coherent. Knowing I have things to take care of in the future keeps me active in the present. And that extends to the people, creatures, and not-sentient-but-still-living things that depend on me. I may not have kids to read to at night anymore, but I've got a dog that loves to play tug-of-war and a bevy of houseplants that would all crumble to dust if I didn't water them. Obviously in the teeth of severe depressive episodes, these small duties feel pointless and worthless. Their call may be drowned by the static in our heads. And yet, even when I was agonizing through my rodeo wipeout, my plants still survived somehow. In that really dark season in my life, my philodendrons still demanded that I dump a little water into their pots every now and then. And so, somehow, I did.*

Responsibilities and relationships, even small responsibilities and relationships, can help egg us on to our literal tomorrows. When we feel needed, we tend to respond.

LOOK UP, NOT DOWN

When I was a kid and my parents would take me and my sister hiking, we'd start off in fine form. We'd gallop through the forests on our pretend horses or fight off pretend orcs with imaginary swords. We'd not so much hike as fly through the Colorado mountains.

At first.

But invariably a mile or two in, we'd forget the game. And by the time we were nearing the end of the hike, I wasn't playing anymore. I wasn't even looking up. Instead of soaking in the beautiful scenery all around us—the trees and mountains and weird-looking rocks—I'd be staring at the red-brown trail in front of me, watching the toes of my boots shoot, metronome-like, into my field of vision with each step.

It's natural, I think. And sometimes looking down is absolutely necessary when you're hiking. You've got to be wary of unexpected rocks or divots in the ground that might just grab your sole. But you don't go into the mountains to just look at dirt for several hours. You go out to see God's creation. Even today when I hike,

---

* I even was gifted a few more, now that I think about it. After I'd missed a couple of weeks, the rodeo headquarters thoughtfully sent me a pot with several live plants in it. All of them are still alive. One tiny ficus plant, which stood about six inches tall and boasted all of a dozen leaves, is now about fifteen feet high. When Christmas comes, we hang lights on it.

I still sometimes find myself looking down more than I should. And the longer and harder the hike, all the more likely it is that I'll get lost in the monotony, the step-by-step journey, and forget the reasons I'm hiking in the first place. I literally lose sight of the beauty all around me.

Those of us who are afflicted with depression invariably— without exception, I think—do the same thing, mentally and emotionally. We feel that our worlds have grown smaller, are sequestered to the equivalent of a ribbon of dirt. Every step looks much the same as the last one you took. You know that 50, 100, 1,000 steps into the future, they'll look the same, too. No wonder life can feel pointless and meaningless when that's our view. No wonder we're inclined to despair.

But it's because we've forgotten, or lost the ability, to look up.

Life is a thing of beauty. All created things—you and I, the towering mountains, and the humble flowers—are the products of unimaginable engineering and poetry and care. We are surrounded by little miracles. We are serenaded by the angels of life every day. And when we see what life truly holds, it can take our breath away.

I know what some of you might be saying. *I do look up. I see the trees and they all look the same. I look at the mountains and they've lost their color. Forward, back, north, south . . . it's all a forest . . . a dark forest with no color, no exit, no hope of escape.*

Reminds me of the first few lines of a famous poem:

Midway upon the journey of our life
I found myself within a forest dark,
For the straightforward pathway had been lost.[22]

So says Dante Alighieri at the outset of *The Divine Comedy*, a poetic trilogy that begins with Inferno, his allegorical journey to hell. Even before he's attacked by three wild beasts, Dante finds this forest incredibly oppressive. "Death could scarce be more bitter than that place!" he tells us,[23] and when the beasts come—a lion, a panther, and a she-wolf—things grow even more dire.

But then, Dante looks up.

And up the sun was mounting with those stars
That with him were, what time the Love Divine
At first in motion set those beauteous things;
So were to me occasion of good hope.[24]

None of the tools I've outlined in this chapter is a miracle pill. These are disciplines that might help you find the road out of the forest dark, and I think they'll help you stay on that road once you've found it. But some forests are darker than others. If you're depressed, seek help and guidance from a professional. Therapy and medication have shown to be incredibly effective tools in fighting depression, especially when used together.

But even the best of psychologists and the most effective medication won't work unless you actively help them work—engaging the world and all its beasts with an active stance, not a passive one. No pills, no matter how good they are, will magically lift you to a better place. But they may give you the wherewithal to walk there yourself.

Look forward. Look outward. Look up. Look toward hope. Toward faith. Toward love and toward God. Therein lies our salvation. It can be hard to see. But we have to try.

CHAPTER 9

DARK NIGHT

I said to my soul, be still, and wait. . . .
So the darkness shall be the light, and the stillness the dancing.

T.S. ELIOT

I WONDER SOMETIMES if the whole world might not be depressed.

Separation is the cause of so much sorrow. In *The Hitchhiker's Guide to the Galaxy*, author Douglas Adams hints at this when he gives an intimate look at how homesick his star-hopping character Ford Prefect is. All life forms, during times of great stress, send off a signal that "simply communicates an exact and almost pathetic sense of how far that being is from the place of his birth,"[1] Adams writes. "On Earth it is never possible to be farther than sixteen thousand miles from your birthplace, which really isn't very far, so such signals are too minute to be noticed. Ford Prefect was at this moment under great stress, and he was born six hundred light-years away."

Perhaps 16,000 miles away isn't much in Adams's world. But ultimately, I believe, our home isn't here: It's with God. If we are indeed His creation, even the most secular and unbelieving of us feel how wrong the world is. How far away He feels. Six hundred light-years is nothing compared to the distance that sin can create between God and us.

And we seem to be getting farther.

God seemed nearer once. God walked in the Garden with Adam and Eve. Abraham ate with Him. Jacob wrestled with Him.[*] By Moses' time, though, God tended to come in other guises: burning bushes and pillars of cloud. When Moses demanded to see God's face, the Lord told him he couldn't and live. By the time of Ezekiel, only the very holy saw Him, and then only in super-weird visions. When God actually came to earth in mortal form—a form we could see and touch and understand—our separation was such that only a very few recognized Him, and even that took time. And even when they learned the truth, Jesus' closest friends often seemed to forget.

The rest of human history seems like a bunny-hop-like procession away from our real home: Like Ford Prefect in *The Hitchhiker's Guide*, we fly ever farther. We embrace our worldly analgesics, hang on to our towels, and stop even trying to find God in anything.

Jesus and Paul both talked about uncovering life in a dead world—*literal* life after literal death, yes, but also new life now in a place that sometimes feels half dead already, blind and deaf and . . . *numb*.

I think that's one reason why people of faith seem to deal with depression less frequently than the secular world: They've experienced the life God promised and, thus, are more resistant to the death the world brings.

---

[*] John 1:18 says pretty definitively that no mortal ever has actually "seen" God, which has made a lot of these stories where people say they *did* see the Almighty a matter of hot theological debate. I was always taught that Jacob's grappling partner was an angel, which a lot of theologians back. Other experts think it was a pre-incarnation version of Jesus, and John Calvin believed it was just a vision. But for the sake of the illustration, let's push on.

But when Christians *do* become depressed, we feel confused and hurt—maybe even a little betrayed. *Where's this living water I was promised, huh?* We know Jesus, just like we're supposed to. We expect to feel more keenly that new life Paul talked about. Instead, we often still feel a little . . . dead. We can be blind to the beauty around us. Deaf to the advice of those who would help us. Numb to joy and fun and, sometimes, even pain and sorrow. God can feel very far away indeed.

It reminds me again of Dante's *Inferno* and the author's trek through the underworld. Squint a little, and the creative punishments Dante finds on his trip through hell's nine circles can feel a little bit like a journey through depression.

In the second circle, the tortured souls are blown by a mighty wind, which to me represents the "static" I sometimes feel, the inability to concentrate. The third circle houses sinners wallowing in a putrid mess of rot, unable to enjoy the food that so consumed them in life. Those in the fourth circle drag around heavy weights. Most anyone with depression can talk about the "weights" they carry. Even the thought of dragging yourself into the shower can plunk what feels like another hundred pounds on your back.

And then, in the ninth circle, we find the great frozen lake of Cocytus, its sinners locked in ice. The nearer Dante and his guide, Virgil, walk toward the center, where Satan himself is trapped, the more they find its inhabitants covered in the stuff. Eventually, they reach sinners who are frozen up to their eyeballs, so even their tears turn to ice before they can be shed. Here, even the solace of crying is not attainable.

I think back to the coldness I felt back in college, back during that dark night when I felt nothing. Some with depression feel like they live in that ninth circle. Or, at least, they make too frequent visits. Locked in ice, they don't feel grief or sorrow. It seems as though all that makes people truly alive has been taken from them, even the pain. The breathing deadness envelops them like the skin of Cocytus.

Here, on that frozen lake, Dante's suffering masses are, literally and spiritually, as far from God as they could be. For them there is no hope. And when Christians feel a little like Dante's wretched sinners, stuck in a frozen lake of depression, it all feels so unfair that we, too, might lose hope. *We don't deserve this!* we think. And often, we've got a point. We're all sinners, of course, but Dante's icebound transgressors committed vile acts of treachery. Plus, we're supposed to be *saved*. So what are we doing on ice? We look up and see nothing, and so we begin to believe (even if we don't say so) that there's nothing above us.

But we depressed types *do* have hope. And maybe we find that in Dante, too. After all, it's here on the frozen lake where the poet stops descending and begins his ascent to heaven—climbing upward on Satan's own back.

Of course, first we have to shake free of the ice.

FAITH IS A CHOICE

That's a hard climb to make, especially when you can't see your terminus. Before he went down to hell, Dante, in his dark forest, could still see the heavens, if not heaven, and what he saw up there gave him hope. Down in the pit of depression, we struggle to see that far. We can't feel the warmth of God's love in that icy place. We have no assurance that God's even there.

I get that low sometimes. I've believed and loved God for most of my life, and I write about Him all the time. But sometimes the silence at the other end of the line can push me into a place of doubt. I struggle with all the same 3 a.m. questions that you probably do. And while I don't think depression is the cause of those doubts and questions, it certainly can make them louder.

When I find myself in that place, sooner or later I'll be reminded of another pit—the one that a pair of English children (Eustace and Jill) and a strange, gangly creature called a Marsh-wiggle (Puddleglum by name) found themselves in during C. S. Lewis's Chronicles of Narnia book *The Silver Chair*.

The Silver Chair is my favorite Narnia novel, perhaps because it so boldly deals with doubt and deception and unsexy sins like laziness. And toward the end of it, Jill, Eustace, and Puddleglum—on a mission to rescue Rilian, the crown prince of Narnia—find themselves deep, deep underground, in the kingdom of the beautiful, beguiling Emerald Witch. She tries to enchant them out of their quest, throwing strange incense in a fire and playing a lute ever so lovingly, telling them that the world above ground and everything in it (including the great lion Aslan, Lewis's avatar of Christ) is just a dream, a childish imagining to be put aside for the dowdier-but-real world they're now in.

It almost works until Puddleglum stands up, walks over to the fire and stamps it out with his bare webbed feet (leaving the room smelling, Lewis writes, much less like magic and incense and much more like burnt Marsh-wiggle). And then Puddleglum says (in part) this:

> Suppose we *have* only dreamed, or made up, all those things—trees and grass and sun and moon and stars and Aslan himself. Suppose we have. Then all I can say is that, in that case, the made-up things seem a good deal more important than the real ones. Suppose this black pit of a kingdom of yours *is* the only world. Well, it strikes me as a pretty poor one. . . . We're just babies making up a

game, if you're right. But four babies playing a game can make a play-world which licks your real world hollow. That's why I'm going to stand by the play-world. I'm on Aslan's side even if there isn't any Aslan to lead it. I'm going to live as like a Narnian as I can even if there isn't any Narnia.[2]

And that's where I land, even when I doubt. When I'm in my pit, when all that I honor and value and love can feel, in the moment, like make-believe, I still stand with Aslan.

As Lewis knew, Puddleglum has every reason to believe. Faith, after all, should never be *blind* faith: It needs to be informed by fact. But this isn't an apologetics book (a book that, essentially, sets down some of those facts), so I won't dwell on that here but instead will let other, much smarter people than me talk about it elsewhere.* Here, I will just say that for many of us, doubts are an inescapable, and some would say, essential part of our walk with God.[3] In another book with, alas, fewer witches and Marsh-wiggles (*Mere Christianity*), Lewis writes:

Now Faith . . . is the art of holding on to things your reason has once accepted, in spite of your changing moods. For moods will change, whatever view your reason takes. I know that by experience now that I am a Christian I do have moods in which the whole thing looks very improbable: but when I was an atheist I had moods in which Christianity looked terribly probable. This rebellion of your moods against your real self

---

* A few of my favorites include G. K. Chesterton's *Orthodoxy*, a clever, logical, and wildly fun illustration of why faith makes sense; C. S. Lewis's *Mere Christianity*; and lots of stuff by Lee Strobel. *The Language of God*, by Nobel-winning scientist Francis S. Collins, is a great book for the more scientifically inclined. And, for philosophy majors, Anthony Flew's *There Is No A God* is a pretty interesting read too.

is going to come anyway. That is why Faith is such a necessary virtue: unless you teach your moods "where they get off," you can never be either a sound Christian or even a sound atheist, but just a creature dithering to and fro, with its beliefs really dependent on the weather and the state of digestion.[4]

Here's the uncomfortable truth behind that statement: Faith is, in some respects, *work*. That's why they call the stuff we do to deepen our faith spiritual *disciplines*. And you have to be disciplined to do them.

Now, some people may engage in those spiritual disciplines with a great deal of joy, just like some people enjoy running. Well, you know now how I feel about running. And yeah, that (ahem) enthusiasm carries over to my spiritual life sometimes. Honestly, I love thinking about God, learning about God, talking about God. But talking *to* God? Going to church? These are things I sometimes have to make myself do. Feel free to judge me, but I'd wager I'm not the only Christian out there who sometimes feels this way.

But I still do these things (at least most of the time) just like I run (most of the time), because I know they're good for me. They keep me healthy, spiritually speaking. And good spiritual health is one of the best defenses for depression I know. And naturally, you need to start with this.

PRAY

A friend of mine gets up every morning at 4:30 or 5 to pray. He spends a full hour in prayer, combing through his prayer journal and talking to God about each person and petition listed—crossing some requests off his list when they've been answered, adding others as they come up. This man has prayed for me and my family, by name, for a dozen years.

He's a joyful runner as well, perhaps not so coincidentally.

He's amazing. And I'd love to follow his example. But I just don't have that kind of time.

That may be a ridiculous statement: *If it's important, you can find the time*, you might be thinking, and that's true. My friend would probably tell me the same thing. I find time for plenty of less worthwhile activities. But I'm telling you where I *am*, not where I'd *like* to be. Finding time to pray is tough for many of us, I think.

I'm not talking about when you bow your heads in church or say grace over meals. Those are nice and all, and I'm sure that God appreciates hearing from you in any circumstance, even if you say a quick prayer at a stoplight. To me, they feel like little texts to heaven, or postcards maybe, when people actually wrote postcards. "Hi God, thanks for everything," we say. And in so many words, we add, "Wish you were here."

But relationships—at least my relationships—require real conversations sometimes. And when it comes to conversing with God, I think, we have to be in the right brain space. Our distractions are legion, and the noise around us is deafening—not very conducive to a reflective heart-to-heart. Sometimes, the prayers we pray at our Christian ministry can feel as much for each other as for God. Sometimes, they take on the tang of performance. And almost always, they're said in between meetings and deadlines and work, work, work—which makes it hard for me to really concentrate on whom we're supposed to be praying to.

When I pray for even two minutes, my mind tends to wander: I fret about deadlines or worry over an old argument. If I'm being forced to hold someone's hand, most of my energy is spent in obsessive attention to that hand, and mine: *Am I clenching? Is my hand sweaty?* If I pray, it's often that God would keep my hand from shaking. And when you're dealing with depression, the static can be especially loud. Sometimes, as I said in the first chapter, my mind pulls me in darker directions during prayer.

It's almost like my mind needs a little prep time, a little warm-up, just like the body warms up during a run.

So, I guess, it just makes sense for me to pray when I run.

Praying while running makes sense. First, what *else* am I gonna do while running? Talking with God helps me pass the time. But second and more importantly, running helps my mind relax. With a little part of my brain focused on keeping me pounding through the predawn streets, the rest of my gray matter doesn't distract or obsess quite so easily. Admittedly, some runs are more conducive to prayer than others: I can still get distracted, especially if a car lunges at me out of nowhere. But I find that running, especially running outdoors in God's creation, helps me feel like I'm connecting a little bit better.

You don't need to sign up for a marathon to improve your prayer life. But I do find *moving prayer*—not prayers that move you deeply, but praying while you're actually moving—actually boosts my sense of connection to heaven. The reception feels a bit sharper in the open air. While some people will swear (though not literally, because that would be bad) by their prayer closets or war rooms or isolated quiet times, I find that praying while doing *something*—not anything that takes any real concentration, but something that gets your body moving and encourages your mind to settle—can be really helpful. Maybe that something for you is folding clothes or painting a bureau or driving to work. Maybe it's just taking a walk in the park. But for me, just as I've found running can loosen the tongue for me and my running partners, so it can help boost my dialogue with God.

I also think we should remember that, as holy as we may feel when we pray, it's at least in part a *selfish* act. I think God asks us to pray not so much because *He* needs it, but because *we* need it. He can come to us at any time, but God knows how we're built: That concentrating and verbalizing and, often, going through the quiet liturgy of prayer helps us move closer to Him. Every facet of prayer, when you think about it, hits on the elements we talked about in the last chapter.

When we give God thanks for all the things in our lives that we're grateful for (or, at least, we know we *should* be grateful for), it helps us to look up, not down—to recognize and honor the beauty in our lives and, in so doing, better understand that those gifts should not be diminished or discarded. When we pray for others, it helps us focus outward, not inward, acknowledging that we're not the only ones who could use some help. And when we pray for God to help us in the midst of depression, we're leaning on a relationship—our relationship with God. We're acknowledging that we can't suffer through this stuff all alone, even though the condition may make us feel like we're all alone.

God listens to us. God cares. But even if you don't feel God speaking to you in the midst of your prayers and you're in the midst of a period of cynicism and doubt, prayer still brings with it some truly tangible benefits. The more you pray, the more your mind will focus on more productive ways to deal with your depression. And as time goes on, you might be surprised that, during some of your prayers, you'll feel God with you. You'll feel not just the comfort that comes with expressing gratitude and processing problems in a meditative manner, but also the comfort of God's holy hand.

GIVE

We have three things we can typically give: our money, our time, and our talents. But because we live in a pretty materialistic society, we often whittle the idea of "giving" to just the first. Here in twenty-first-century America, most of us are relatively lazy and relatively rich: Dropping twenty bucks in the offering plate or shipping a monthly donation to the charity of our choice is a fairly simple way for us to all feel a little better about ourselves.

And make no mistake, that sort of giving helps. It really does. The ministry I work for would go belly up if it weren't for those donations, so keep sending that money, people!*

But when it comes to depression, and in treating the spiritual side of those afflicted with it, I think money might be the least effective method of giving I know of. It is simply too passive. Passivity can be a great friend of depression: For me, passivity helped pull me into it. Reacting too passively to that depression kept me depressed. No, better to give *actively* to others as a form of treatment. Give something of yourself, not just your paycheck.

We talked about how important it can be to take on reasonable amounts of responsibility—to give yourself reasons to get up in the morning. Sometimes that equates to jobs and careers and such, but for some depressed people, jumping into a busy workplace can quickly move from reasonable responsibility to unreasonable levels of stress—at least at first. (And if your depression has kept you out of work for a while—and keep in mind, it is the leading cause of disability in the United States[5]—getting a job at first might be a little tricky anyway.)

Volunteering for a church or charity can help ease you back into accepting and handling responsibility—say, for just a couple

---

* You're more than welcome to send me donations directly too.

of hours a week at first. And as your responsibilities grow, I think you'll find that your ability to enjoy what you're doing increases too. It helps you foster relationships—and those relationships will be with, theoretically, some pretty good, caring people who share your same concerns for the world around us. Wring your hands over the environment? Volunteering for a Christian eco-group (and yes, people, they do exist) will connect you with people who love nature. Have a heart for the elderly? Teach kids? Feed the hungry? Care for animals? I know of countless local and national organizations that can help facilitate these things. And I've never seen a church that couldn't use some extra help.

And while volunteering doesn't pay as well as, y'know, *working*, it comes with an oft-overlooked benefit: Volunteers, if they're volunteering for something they believe in and care about, go home with a sense of accomplishment—that they're using their time to make the world a better, healthier, more positive place. Often, you're impacting lives directly, and impacting them for the better. Accountants and sales managers and grocery-store clerks might not always feel that sort of immediate fulfillment.

Psychologists know that volunteering can be really effective in treating depression.[6] I mean, really effective. A story written for *Vice* called it mental health's "Best Kept Secret," and author Kaleigh Rogers says that her own volunteer work has helped immeasurably with her depression. "Volunteering is one of the most self-serving things I do," she writes, "because whenever I help out at the horse barn, my stress and anxiety levels noticeably drop. I feel calmer, more relaxed, and my mind is clear, often for the first time in weeks. It has quickly become one of the most reliable ways for me to de-stress—I've found it more effective than meditation, medication, or exercise."[7]

Sometimes, the best way to help yourself is to help someone

else. If we all remembered that more often, the world would be a better place.

GO TO CHURCH

Confession time: I hate church a little.

Blame part of it on my introversion. Churches—particularly evangelical churches—are designed for extroverts, what with their raised hands and happy worship music and their (ugh) let's-greet-the-people-sitting-next-to-you routine. If I were to design a church service for depressed introverts, it'd consist of a sermon, a time of reflection, and songs filled not with hallelujahs, but bittersweet laments. Oh, and all the congregants would be sitting in separate cubicles.

But it's not entirely my fault that I don't like church. Church sometimes bears a bit of the responsibility too.

Back in chapter 3, I mentioned that my own experience in church as a child was a little rough around the edges. But I think many churchgoers know that the House of the Almighty sometimes feels a little more like a House of Arguments. When I was a religion reporter, I attended probably hundreds of churches and got to know pretty well some of those who ran them and worked in them, and I saw and heard plenty of friction. Think our national political system can get petty and vile? Check out your average midsize congregation when it comes time to replace the sanctuary carpet. Churches often do some incredibly wonderful things, but the most valuable service they sometimes provide is to show us that we are *all* sinners in need of grace—not just from God, but from each other. And sometimes the most churched of us can use the most grace.

Occasionally the church—not God's holy ideal of the church, but the man-made, misshapen thing we sometimes twist it into—can inflict deep wounds. I'm not the only kid who had a bad experience in church. I've interviewed men who were abused by priests when they were children, women harassed by pastors, pastors unfairly torn down by their own flock. We have such high ideals for the church and its leaders that, when they reveal themselves as less than ideal—and sometimes much, *much* less—the cuts can go that much deeper. To be slugged in the face by a stranger, that's one thing. But to be slugged in the face by a friend? Someone you trusted? So much more painful that can be.

I won't downplay the faults we sometimes can find in church. But here's the thing: As imperfect as it can be, the church can still be, and often is, beautiful. Sometimes the pettiest of churches can be the prettiest, too. We sometimes have to squint to see it, but it's there. And, I believe, that particular form of beauty can only be found there—in a body of believers who might not agree on the color of the carpet, but who look up to the heavens and sing and pray together anyway.

God meant for us to worship Him, and gather, in community. Verse after verse after verse tells us so. That community, if you find the right one, can be critical for someone who's depressed. The affliction is so inherently isolating. It drives you away from friends, makes it hard to work, pushes you away from many traditional support networks. And while not every church will understand how to intersect with depression, the folks inside do know about pain. They hopefully understand that they're there to help. They *want* to help.

In addition, the ritual we find in church—even evangelical churches that make it a point to stress how nontraditional they are—can be a salve to the anxious mind. I talked about how important routine was in my own mental health, and ritual is nothing more than formalized routine. Again, I don't think God necessarily cares how many songs we sing before the sermon or when exactly the announcements land, but we do. The familiar pattern of worship can settle the static in us, even cleanse us, to some extent, of the anxiety and worry we bring in. It's a little like those moving prayers, perhaps: When a bit of you engages in ritual, the rest of you can better concentrate on what really matters. You can think about the One you've come to church to honor and consider and celebrate.

Go to an old-school church—one with an actual steeple and stuff—and you might find a red door. It's especially common on Episcopal churches, I believe, but other denominations sport it too. Google "red door church," and you'll see hundreds, maybe thousands of them. The color isn't just a jaunty decor decision: It holds deep meaning.

Perhaps it extends back to Passover, when the Hebrews were instructed to paint blood on their doorposts—a signal to the Lord to pass on by.[8] The color is intended to symbolize Christ's blood, too, and the sacrifice that made the church itself possible and viable.[9] For centuries, it was a promise of sanctuary—that someone, no matter how scared or hurt or troubled, could find safety within its walls.

Not all churches have red doors anymore. But any church worth its spiritual salt should still be a place of safety for those of us hurting, despairing, and looking for hope.

SEEK OUT THE THIN PLACES

I first heard the term "thin places" when I was a religion writer at *The Gazette.* The term comes from Celtic Christianity (some believe the term is older than that), and it points to places where believers felt the veil between heaven and earth was particularly fine. Those two realms of heaven and earth, a Celtic saying insists, are just three feet apart anyway. But in a thin place, the distance between the two grows narrower yet, becoming almost translucent.[10]

I've never been to a "formal" thin place that the Celtics recognized as such, like the island of Iona or craggy Croagh Patrick. But living in Colorado, I think I can appreciate the term a little more than some. The air here is literally thinner than it is most places. And in the mountains—the High Country, as some call it around here—heaven can sometimes feel close enough to touch.

I have no idea what heaven will look like, but I'd imagine it'd smell like pine trees.

But I don't think that thin places are necessarily bound by geography. They're not like holes in the ozone layer, hovering above Iona or Colorado's Maroon Bells. With a poke of a finger, God makes His own thin places sometimes, pushing into the membrane between Him and us like we would the skin of a balloon. It can happen anywhere, and it often takes us by surprise. But paradoxically, it helps if we set the table a bit—if we consciously try to move closer to Him.

I think that the three elements I discussed can become catalysts to create those thin places: We can find them in prayer. In church. When we're giving of our time and talents. And sometimes, just thinking about God can seemingly bring us closer to the door of the holy.

I've said that I've seldom felt the presence of God tangibly in my life. But I didn't say I never have. I feel Him—or perhaps more fairly, a desire to be close to Him—when I'm singing. Sometimes in the early morning as I pray, I run over a ridge and see the sun bathe the city in pink and orange, and I feel as though I'm in the presence of something deeply, unfathomably holy.

Depression can make it more difficult to feel those thin places. The veil between heaven and earth feels far away indeed when it feels like you're a hundred miles under the earth, when you find yourself deep in that pit.

But even then, I think, God can reach us. His reach is long. His love is broad. Even Cocytus is not too far.

I was driving home from *The Gazette* one evening. I was years past my rodeo wipeout, my last severe depressive episode. But over the last few days I'd found myself slipping into a lower, more difficult frame of mind. I'd had some hard conversations with a friend of mine, and through them—not through his fault, but through my own convicted sense of self—I was pretty down. I felt, powerfully, a sense of worthlessness, a sense of deep angst at the gulf between who I should be and who I was.

And then, it seemed as though God pulled apart the heavens and allowed me, for a moment, to glimpse something about Him. Not His face or His back. There was no burning bush or pillar of smoke. The English language is a beautiful, versatile tool, but I have no words that can convey that moment. Perhaps no language could. But I know the moment was so powerful that I literally pulled the car to the side of the road, to be sucked up as if by tractor beam by the thin place I'd just found.

When I was seven, I'd imagined that my pastor spoke of a God who would send us all to the cross before He would embrace us. He exacted a staggering entrance fee, I imagined back then. And though I'd been taught otherwise in the decades since—I knew, rationally, that that couldn't be true—it's hard to shake the lessons of childhood. The image of the cross, of me on that cross, still had a place in my soul. Like a burr, it stuck.

In that moment, I had a powerful thought—not conscious but there. Whether it was a sudden realization in my own psyche or whether God was speaking to me (perhaps a thin silence in that thin place), I cannot say. But here it was.

"Be still, and know that I am God," the psalmist writes in Psalm 46:10. *Be still.*

I was still. I think I felt a little like Job in that moment—chastened, but beautifully so, humbled in my awe. What if I had to suffer to find heaven? What if God asked for a hard sacrifice? In that moment, I thought, *what of it?* My only hope was to find myself in God's hand, if only for an instant. What God did with me once I was there was beside the point. I wanted to be there with Him. That was it. That was all.

Eventually I started up the car and went home again. But in that moment, something changed in me. I still feel worthless and weak sometimes, but it comes with the context of that moment—to know the truth of my insignificance, and yet the glory of it, too, to be so unworthy and yet somehow precious. To be so twisted and yet so treasured.

As hard as depression can be, I wonder if sometimes it comes with a certain advantage. We feel more deeply, I think, how far away from God we are. We understand how broken we are. When we approach God, we have nothing to offer. We can bring only our sad, pitiful, hurting selves. We come as beggars. We have barely the strength to knock on heaven's door.

But when it opens—and I believe this with all my heart—we will feel its warmth. The coldness of the pit we've lived in for so long will flake away. And all of us—no matter our illnesses or afflictions or our states of mind—will feel what it means to be loved as we never have before.

CHAPTER 10

THE DRAGON

If you're going through hell, keep going.

WINSTON CHURCHILL

THE DRAGON WAS BEAUTIFUL, maybe the most beautiful thing I'd ever seen.

It was covered in purple and green scales. Its eyes stared wide and wild, and fire cascaded out of its mouth. Its head was printed on a circle of plastic strapped to a plastic frame, and its plastic tail stretched behind it like a Christmas ribbon. To six-year-old me, it looked thirty feet long.

Cartoons told me that kites were modest, diamond-shaped things with a string of bows for a tail. Sometimes they'd get eaten by trees. This kite seemed very different and too magnificent for words. And soon, my dad told me, we'd make it fly.

We went out one breezy afternoon and, after a couple of false starts, successfully launched it into the white-speckled blue. I watched as it soared and swooped above our heads, going higher and higher. And then I took my eyes off the dragon and started paying attention to the string.

Dad slowly unfurled the fishing wire turn by turn. The string was so thin, almost invisible. He encouraged me to take hold of the spool and touch the string, so I could feel it pull. It felt so taut that it seemed possible to pluck it, like a guitar string. How could such a powerful dragon be held with such a tiny thread? What if it broke? What if the string ran out? Already the dragon was impossibly high to me—high enough to touch passing planes or vanish in the clouds. What if we couldn't bring it back?

I don't remember what happened next, but I imagine I started to cry.

My dad remembers that afternoon too. When he tells the story, he asked why I hated flying the kite so much.

"I feel like I'm flying, with the kite," he remembers me saying.

I'm sure I did say that, and I think that was at least partly true. Somehow, it felt like the kite pulled up a section of my soul with it. And as the kite danced in the wind, I imagined myself looking from its dizzying viewpoint—my dad looking as tiny to it as the kite looked to me.

But as I think back, I remember more the fear I had, watching the eyelash-thin string clinging to that elegant, powerful dragon. Only that string kept it tethered to earth. To *us*. If it pulled free—as it so clearly wanted to—it'd be gone forever. I imagined it floating up and up and up, finally vanishing into the blue—all alone in that big, cold sky, and then gone forever. Taking, maybe, that little piece of me with it.

Loving someone with mental illness can feel like that. We see their beauty, their grace. But they pull and twist, and sometimes it feels like we're powerless to bring them back. As hard as we try to reel them back to us, they pull away—winding into the high unknown, farther and farther from our love and help.

I watched the heart monitor sink lower, lower.

The prenatal counselors warned us that something like this might happen. Lots of things happen in the womb, they said. The umbilical cord can wrap around the child's neck. The baby can be in the wrong position. Each contraction can add to the stress. Doctors will monitor the baby's heart rate throughout the birth, and it's possible that the heart rate could drop—sometimes significantly. A normal rate of 160 beats a minute can sink to 40 during contractions. Maybe 30. Maybe lower.

I remembered all this as I held Wendy's hand and watched the heart rate of our baby—the baby who we'd name Colin—sink. From 160, it sank to 40. Then 30.

Then it rallied. Back to 80, 120. He was fine. I forced myself to smile gently, reassuring Wendy that everything was fine. And it was.

I hoped it was.

She couldn't see the heart rate monitor. The doctor and nurses could, and they didn't seem overly worried. And all of them were, as you might imagine, preoccupied. My only job was to be with Wendy and coach her on her breathing. And so I watched the baby's heartbeat to pass the time: a living being, about to come and see the world.

Another contraction hit. 30 beats. Then 12. Then 4. Then back to normal. He's just fine, I said. *Will he be fine?* I wondered.

Another contraction. 20 beats. 8 beats. 2.

Nothing.

The zero glowed green and horrible. Two full seconds passed before it came back.

I've prayed often, of course: reasoned, rational prayers—thanking

God for all His many blessings, petitioning for this thing or that, apologizing for my latest mistake.

We pray differently when it's the only hope we have.

I had no idea whether those dips in the heart rate were faults in the machine. Maybe they were relatively normal or really, really not. I hoped they were normal. I was terrified that they were not. I prayed like a man under the shadow of enemy bombers, prayed like the last man on the *Titanic* watching the last lifeboat lower.

Please God, I shouted silently, still trying to smile. *Please, let my baby live.*

Moments later, the doctor whipped out what some affectionately call the salad tongs. One last pull, one last push, and Colin was with us. Crying.

The tongs pinched a nerve. To this day, part of his lower lip sags when he smiles—a crooked grin matched with a laugh I still never tire of hearing.

When Colin was about five years old, a family friend of ours asked Colin if he was scared of the dark.

"No," Colin somberly told him as he walked away. "It's the things *in* the dark that scare me . . ."

Colin has always been a curious mix of logic and imagination— a scientist with an artist's soul. He walked before he crawled, and while he was late to talk, he spoke in complete sentences from almost the beginning.

"Truck!" he said one day in his car seat, pointing at an SUV.

"Very good, Colin!" I told him, impressed with his deduction and encouraged by his word use.

"Actually, it's a minivan," he said.

We all live in a world of paradox, but he seems made of them: so cynical, yet so believing. Liberal yet archly conservative. He thrives with order but embraces chaos. I remember him cowering when he heard the lions roar at the zoo. Then a few days later, I'd find him throwing pillows and blankets out of his second-story window, prepping for a spectacular jump. As an adult, he jumped out of a moving car because he didn't care for the conversation. He still has the scars. And yet he's willing to spend hours with a sick or scared friend, caring for him or her like a mother would. When Wendy stepped on a stingray in Florida one year, it was Colin who cared for her, running hot water over her foot until the pain went away.

It's the things in the dark I'm scared of, he said.

Me too.

Several months ago, when Colin was in a particularly dark place, he seemed to be trying to warn me of something. He didn't understand how some people, parents especially, thought love was defined by never letting go. He wondered why parents thought it was such a beautiful thing to pursue their children to the ends of the earth to "save" them, whether they needed saving or not. Or even if they did need saving, they so clearly didn't want to be saved.

"Why can't they let go?" he said.

He doesn't understand how much it means to me that he's with us at all—how hard I prayed for his safe arrival, how much I've prayed for him every day since. He can't know what it's like to be a parent and experience the insanity that the job often comes with.

"Love is merely a madness," Shakespeare once wrote,[1] and perhaps he was right. Love is rarely reasonable. And outside God's love for us, a parent's love might be the most unreasonable of all. It comes with a bevy of excesses: We may trust without grounds for trusting; we may push beyond the bounds for pushing. Our love and the myriad dysfunctional ways we can show it has bought many a psychologist's yacht, I'm sure.

But I'm a dad. Holding on is what I do—as long as I can, to the ends of my strength.

But it's not easy. And when you love someone who suffers from mental illness, be it depression or anxiety or something else, holding on can sometimes feel as though you're holding on not to the end of a kite, but a real dragon—one who thrashes and pulls and, sometimes, threatens to yank you from firm ground and carry you with him.

It was the Monday after Easter, and Colin was in sixth grade. I had talked with him that morning, like I almost always did. I was getting ready to leave for work, and I asked him to take out the trash before he caught the school bus.

A couple of hours later, my phone buzzed. It was Wendy. The school called, she said, and Colin hadn't shown up for class. She said she was going home to check. I said to give me a call when she learned anything.

Skipping? I thought. Not like Colin. He never skipped. Never missed school. He was such a good kid.

Then Wendy called back. At first I couldn't understand her, she was crying so hard.

"He ran away!" She sobbed.

I raced home and read Colin's note. He loved us all, it said, but he wasn't happy with how his life was going. He was going to walk to Wendy's parents' house, he wrote, more than 100 miles away. He apologized for taking $40 from our room. He gave a precious knickknack he'd bought at Disneyland—a coffin full of skulls—to his sister. It felt almost like a will.

He'd taken out the trash before he left.

For the next several hours we searched. The only way he'd ever been to Grandma and Grandpa's was via the interstate, so Wendy and my parents searched along there. Wendy's parents were on high alert, waiting for any calls that might come from Colin or us. I thought Colin might—*might*—try to go a back way, north through the mountains behind our house. I went out and walked, hollering for an hour straight until the owner of the sprawling mountain property buzzed by on an ATV, probably to see who was trespassing. But when he saw my state and heard my story, he encouraged me to hop aboard, and he drove me around.

"He'll be all right," he told me. "Probably just needed to get something out of his system."

I thought about the video games we played together, the cartoons we watched together, the books we read together. I wondered what would happen if we didn't find him. I wondered if I'd ever be able to smile again.

It was pointless, I knew, to look in the woods. It had snowed up in the higher hills, and the trail was empty of tracks. I went back home to think of something else I could do, something that might help.

Funny how these desperate moments with Colin always seem punctuated by digital numbers. In Hastings, Colin's heart rate monitor glowed green. At home, our answering machine glowed red. And instead of a zero, there was a number *1*. It flashed. He'd called.

I learned later that Colin had made it to north Colorado Springs before he was picked up in a fast-food joint by a guy in a truck. The trucker asked him how far he wanted to go. Colin told him he wanted to go up to Longmont, near his grandparents' farm. The man said he'd take him.

But by the time they hit Castle Rock—about halfway to

Longmont—Colin had changed his mind. He wanted to be dropped off at the outlet mall there. And that's where he called from. He was in the food court, he told the answering machine.

"I'm ready to come home."

We took him to a counselor the next day, who said he was just fine. Either she or Colin explained it away as a surge of emotion—a flash flood of adolescent, chemical fight-or-flight response that he didn't have the maturity to deal with.

We wanted it to be true. And maybe it was. We went back to our lives, almost as if nothing happened. A blip. Like the skip of a heartbeat. Nothing more. We tried to forget about it. I've never written about it until now. Wendy had asked me never to do so. Too painful.

But I still remember what Colin told me a few weeks later: how it was the best and worst day of his life, that feeling of utter misery combined with complete freedom.

If I could do it over again—and rarely a week goes by that I don't wish I could—I would've taken him to counseling more than that one time. I would've been more intentional about talking about everything he was thinking and feeling that day.

I never asked whether he was bullied at school. I asked him why he'd been so unhappy, but I bought his explanations and never went further. I never asked more about the truck driver. Perhaps my reticence was the product of depression, but perhaps not. Maybe every father and mother who tries to help a child through some difficult emotional time feels much the same. How could we not, really?

Mothers and fathers are wired to protect their families in their own unique ways. Ever since I had kids, my worst fears were about letting them down, my worst nightmares about being unable to save them. That's the gig, after all—the most crucial duty of fatherhood. To save your kids if they need saving. And that's just great, of course. But we moms and dads are people, too, so we need to feel that we're doing a good job. And when it feels like we're not—well, maybe we all have an urge to protect ourselves and our psyches, too. Like an employee who missed a deadline or missed a goal, we have an instinct to ignore or make excuses or blame someone else for what happened on our watch. And maybe those excuses have all sorts of merit. But sometimes, focusing on those excuses and fixating on our own underlying shame and guilt make it harder to tackle the actual problem. We try to explain away what happened instead of ensuring that the root problem is taken care of—that it'll never happen again.

I wonder whether that was in play after Colin ran away. When Colin seemed just fine in the aftermath, Wendy and I were so relieved and so grateful. We took a few steps to erase what we thought might've been some of the triggers. But when it seemed like everything was just A-OK, we didn't poke or prod too much more. We didn't dare. We loved Colin, and we were so happy when he came back to us—in a physical sense, of course, but also emotionally. He felt like our little boy, and we were so happy.

And don't get me wrong. He *did* come back to us in every way. That was no lie, no weird facade of reunification. But I wonder, looking back, how much we really knew our little boy at all.

I made—and continue to make, when I'm not careful—a dangerous assumption, that Colin is a lot like me. And in a lot of ways he is. But we're all ultimately unique creations of a divine and mysterious Creator. And when it comes to how each of us sees and processes the world around us, such assumptions, as understandable as they are, can be dangerous.

If you're a parent of a child who you think may be anxious or depressed, my advice is very, very simple: *Talk* to your son or daughter. Pry if you have to. Do whatever you can to develop a good talking relationship with your kids—one where they feel they can tell you anything and everything. There will be times that you don't want to hear everything they'll tell you. There may be times when you want to cover your ears like a preschooler, shutting it all out.

Hear it anyway. Be brave. Be strong. Love them through it all.

Several years back, I had a chance to help Jim Daly, president of Focus on the Family, write a book called *The Good Dad*. It was a parenting book, but it wasn't one of those *10 Sure-Fire Steps to Raise Perfectly Wonderful Children* sorts of books. It took a look at what it means to be a real, fallible parent of real, frustrating kids. Jim offered an illustration that impacted me deeply.

I asked him about the sometimes difficult relationship between parent and child. *How do you love your children when they make big mistakes?* I asked. *Reject your advice? How do you preserve the relationships when they move away from you physically? Emotionally? Spiritually?* I didn't know it at the time, but I wasn't just asking about what happens when your kid goes (to use an obnoxiously preachy term) all prodigal on you (though that, too). I was touching, indirectly, on this issue of uniqueness—when you understand, as all parents do eventually (if only occasionally), that your kids aren't the little mini-me's you thought you were raising. They have their own minds and souls that process things much differently than you do, and out of those minds and souls can foster very different ideals and goals and even neuroses.

Jim said that he saw the love between parent and child as something like a tetherball: You're the pole, your child's the ball. Sometimes the ball's so close to the pole that it touches. Sometimes it's soaring far away, and that happens more often as a child grows older and, eventually, grows up. But as long as the tether—the love between parent and child—doesn't break, they'll always be connected somehow.

It's a little like a kite, when you think about it.

I think about that illustration a lot.

I've described my own experience with depression. Dealing with it hasn't been easy. But honestly, watching and worrying about someone I love going through the same sort of thing, only worse, is harder. Much harder, I think. I'd trade places with him if I could. I'd go back—back to the worst of my depression—if I had some guarantee that my sinking into it would pull him out of his own woes forever. He could visit me as I lay on the couch and tell me all about his life.

Ironically, I wouldn't be happy about the trade, because I'd be depressed. Of course. But would I be satisfied? I think I would.

It's a difficult thing, to master the art of metaphorical kite flying. We're wired to protect our children. But we also need to prepare them for their lives—to send them out on their own to fly. To give them the tools to survive and thrive without you when the time comes. That's part of the "protection" racket too. You protect them from unnecessary harm, yes, but you also prepare them for the inevitable difficulties that are to come. You teach them how to protect themselves.

But with mental illness, there's only so much you can do. You can pick a twelve-year-old up at an outlet mall, but you can't pluck despair out of someone's brain.

So I keep an eye on that tether. I try to keep it in good repair, to let Colin know that his mom and I are here for him. We aren't going away. Like the tether pole, we're rooted, and he'll always have a place to circle back to. A place to call home.

"Can you check on Colin?" the text says. "His texts aren't making any sense."

Colin's living at home, that day of the overdose. That afternoon I mowed the lawn, listening to the blast of his music, grumbling under my breath. *Why wasn't he doing this? Why does he insist on playing that trash so loud? Why can't he listen to Simon & Garfunkel? Why won't he grow up?*

But after Wendy reads me the texts, the now familiar fear, almost like nausea, squeezes my lungs, my stomach, my heart. Guilt does, too.

Wendy and I consult with each other briefly. *What are we going to do? What if he doesn't want to talk?* I call downstairs. He answers and we wait. But after five minutes, no Colin. I open the door and trudge, fearfully, down the stairs, preparing myself to drag him up if need be.

He's standing up, buckling his belt around his too-skinny waist. He looks tired, but his eyes dart like waterbugs. He comes up, annoyed but quietly. Wendy starts the interrogation. *Are you all right? Did you take something?*

Long pause.

"Do you know how much aluminum is in the human body?" he counters. He rattles off a few numbers, pulled maybe from ancient textbooks or straight from the air.

"Did you swallow a bunch of aluminum foil?" Wendy asks, calmly.*

Another long pause.

---

* Yes, it was a ludicrous conversation. Weird how some of life's most stressful, most traumatic moments come laced with dialogue that you'd find in a third-rate sitcom.

"Maybe," he says, eyes flickering like the heartbeat of a mosquito. "I don't remember."

We buckle him into the car and drive to the hospital, Wendy sitting in the back seat with Colin just in case he decides to jump out. Once in the emergency room, Colin seems a little more himself. He answers the beefy nurse—he looks like he could be a professional linebacker—with a self-effacing smile. Colin says he'd taken a handful of Benadryl pills, another handful of Ibuprofen.

"Were you trying to kill yourself?" the nurse asks.

It's complicated, Colin says. That afternoon, he was made to feel pretty awful about himself. He needed to escape, he felt. Instead of jumping out of a car, he needed to jump out of life for a bit. The pills offered an escape. Perhaps temporary. Perhaps permanent. Colin wasn't necessarily trying to kill himself, he says. But he wouldn't have minded if he had. "Russian roulette," he said.

We spend the rest of the evening in the hospital's high security ward, temporary home to the insane, the intoxicated, the criminal. The beds are set in a semicircle around the nurse's station, with only gauzy curtains for privacy. Two beds down, a police officer watches over one patient. Nearer, a drunk pleads with the nurses to let him stay. On the other side of us, a social worker quizzes a man who thinks he's literally Satan.

"Are you homicidal?" the social worker asks the man.

"Do you want me to strip for you, c---?" he responds.

Dante's *Inferno* has nothing on a hospital's high-security ward.

Emergency rooms were nothing new to Colin and Wendy. Colin was an athlete with little regard for his body. Casts, X-rays . . . all old hat. But the last time I'd been in the hospital with Colin, he weighed less than five pounds. He came out with a swirl of black hair, scratches on his face, and a crooked mouth. And when I put my finger in his hand, he squeezed it tight. So tight. Like he'd never let go.

How can you help someone who's depressed?

I know some of you *need* those answers—need them, maybe, more than you ever needed anything. Someone you love is hurting. Someone you care for feels, more and more, like a stranger. You feel so powerless, so unequal to the task of easing the pain in front of you, so inadequate in your attempts to show this someone—a friend, a father, a son, a spouse—that the world has hope in it yet.

You don't want to hear what I'm about to say . . . but I need those answers too. Man, what I would give to have them. To give them. The right word at the right time. To know when to love and when (and if) to lecture. To get a promise that everything is really going to be all right—that someday, Colin and I will look back at those days and smile. "Man, wasn't *that* the pits?"

What I would give. What I would do. What I would pay for that guarantee.

But the world is cruel, and God doesn't work that way. I'm so often lost in uncertainty, afflicted by my mistakes. My son's doing better now than he was back then, but we have a ways to go yet before I can say, with confidence, that *it's all behind us. Everything's better*. Every day, I watch for signs of both regression and improvement. Every day, I worry. And as I struggle to discern how best to help, I hear my own depression chuckling, as if prepping for another sequel.

Sleepless nights? Yep. A sense of helplessness and worthlessness? Too true. Makes me wonder sometimes whether God was prepping me for *now*—a little depressive tutorial to get ready for the real test.

Whatever answers I have for you, I think, come hard earned, a product of my own missteps and mistakes. But for whatever they're worth, here they are.

BE THERE

You don't need to have the answers or the right things to say. Just be there. Listen to them cry. Listen to them rage. Hold their hand. Grab tissues for them. Just be there. With an affliction like depression, the isolation can feel so extreme that knowing someone's there—that someone really does give a damn—can make a huge difference.

ENCOURAGE AS MUCH AS YOU'RE ALLOWED

Wendy had the right idea when I was in deep depression. When I was in my rodeo wipeout, she gave me a little space—but she also gave me reasons to get out of that basement. She pushed me to go walking with her. She encouraged me to eat. She reminded me every day how much she loved me, how much I had to live for outside the walls of my basement dungeon.

It's important to remember that the first twenty times she made these overtures, I turned her down cold. *I don't want to walk. I don't want to eat. Leave me alone.* But Wendy never stopped trying. She left me alone, but she never left me imprisoned with myself—never got sick of me and said, *Fine, do whatever you want. I'm done with you.* She would've had every reason to, every excuse. But she didn't.

This can be outrageously difficult to keep at, by the way. We know Einstein famously said about insanity that it's "doing the same thing over and over again and expecting different results."* But when it comes to loving and encouraging someone through depression, that's what we must do to some extent. And again, we've already established that love is a little crazy.

"Attitude, to me, is more important than facts," the great pastor Charles Swindoll once said. "It is more important than the past,

---

* Even though, apparently, someone else actually said it. Says *Business Insider*: "As it turns out, insanity might be crediting that quote to Einstein over and over again."

than education, than money, than circumstances, than failure, than successes, than whatever people think or say or do. . . . We cannot change our past . . . we cannot change the fact that people will act in a certain way. We cannot change the inevitable. The only thing we can do is play on the one string we have, and that is our attitude. I am convinced that life is 10% what happens to me and 90% how I react to it."[2]

After dealing with depression as long as I have, I believe this to be true. We all know the world can be a pretty miserable place. No one's suggesting that we pretend otherwise. But how are we going to deal with it? That's up to us. We need to encourage a sense of hopefulness and cast a vision for the future for our despairing friends and relationships, as much as we can and as gently as we can.

But that said, we need to internalize the next point.

YOU CAN'T DO IT FOR THEM

Here's the hardest lesson of all. Colin was right in a way. Sometimes, you have to let go. We're all meant to fly, even if sometimes we crash a time or two. Sometimes, those crashes are critical parts of us learning to fly better. And none of us can do that if we're locked in a closet.

Don't let go of your love, of course. Don't let go of your determination to care and do whatever you can to help your loved one through his or her depression. But you do have to let go of the notion that, somehow, you can drag your loved one through it. Samwise Gamgee carried Frodo up that mountain for a while, but he couldn't do everything.

Keep that tether in good repair. But be aware that, despite your best intentions, sometimes things fray. Sometimes, even if we do everything we could and should, things break.

Another odd movie illustration: You remember that scene at the end of *Indiana Jones and the Last Crusade*? The Templar shrine holding the Holy Grail is breaking apart because of, y'know, spiritual magic and stuff, and the Grail itself has tumbled down into a gaping crevasse. One person has already fallen to her doom trying to retrieve it. Now Indiana (Harrison Ford), our hero, is hanging over the same chasm—one hand held tightly by his father (Sean Connery), while the other reaches to grasp the cup.

"Indiana," Henry Jones Sr. says, almost in a whisper. "Indiana. Let it go." And so Indy does—turning his face from the Grail, and grabbing his father's hands with his.

The point of this illustration is not to compare depression to the Holy Grail, because that just feels wrong. But it does remind us of one of the hardest, saddest aspects of mental illness: No matter how many people are in place to help, ultimately the will to fight depression must come from the one who is suffering from it. You can't take on that person's pain and despair, as much as you might like to. You can't be held responsible for alleviating it. When I feel like a failure because *Colin* is feeling down . . . maybe that's my own depression talking. And even if it's not, the guilt we feel—*could we say something more? Do something better?*—is wholly unproductive and beside the point. It doesn't help either you or the depressed person move forward.

Free will can be such an inconvenience. We can sometimes make people say things or do things, but we can never make them *believe* things . . . even if we believe it's for their own good.

DON'T LOSE HOPE

A well-meaning Christian once told me that, if you pray for something for thirty days straight, you're bound to get an answer from

God. It doesn't mean God will answer that prayer in the way you'd like, but you'll get an answer.

Even well-meaning Christians aren't always right.

Anyone who's prayed about a rocky marriage, an unsaved parent, or a prodigal child knows that we can pray for people for years, even decades. The issues we struggle with can be stubbornly static, and that's particularly true in the realm of mental illness and affliction. And I admit to sometimes despairing a bit. It's hard not to when you love someone struggling with deep emotional or mental issues, because those issues can be so stubborn. And we wonder if *this*—this miserable spot we share with our loved one, this pit without sight of the stars—will be where we'll sit forever. Whether he, and we, will ever move past it.

If I weren't a Christian, maybe it'd stop right there . . . in doubt. In the cynicism that our lives won't necessarily get better. Cocytus will never thaw.

But the only constant we have, ever, is that something's bound to change. And in God, we must believe that we can change for the better. I go back to the exhortation I made in the very first chapter: Hope isn't a feeling. It's a virtue. We push into hope. We work at hope. And if we truly believe that there is a God and He's who we say He is, there's always room for hope.

And it can be found in surprising places.

That night in the emergency room was, unquestionably, the longest of my life. We were there from nine at night till nine in the morning, and none of us slept.

Because of the slew of pills he'd taken, Colin's heart was beating faster than it did in utero—180 beats a minute, sometimes higher.

He was wired. He'd close his eyes for a couple of minutes and then bolt upright in bed. He'd look for his belongings—his wallet and keys and belt, which they'd taken from him—and fret that he'd never get them back. Sometimes he'd get up and start looking for an unseen bowling alley (he really wanted to go bowling), and Wendy and I would have to lead him gently back to bed. He was hallucinating quite a bit too. He'd see mice run across his covers. He'd smack invisible insects on the bed frame. Every once in a while, he was sure there was a stash of tacos under the bed.

Around 3 a.m., he whispered to me. "Dad," he said. "Look."

He was cupping something invisible in his hands—something obviously precious and delicate, something only he could see. He slowly took his right hand away from whatever it was and motioned for me to come closer. As I leaned in, he grasped my left hand in his right and moved it carefully to where he cupped the invisibility, like a child would hold a parent's hand to bring him or her closer to touch a caterpillar or butterfly.

I put my hand next to his, and slowly, gently, he put the unseen thing in mine. He shaped my hands just so in order to hold it better, to make sure it didn't fly away. He turned to me and smiled a smile I've rarely seen, not for years. A smile that said we were together, sharing a beautiful secret.

It felt, in that moment, like he was twelve again. And he trusted me with the most important thing in the world.

He doesn't remember that moment. I always will. In the midst of that horrible, awful night I was given a moment of painful beauty.

He doesn't remember what he saw. But I know what he dropped into my cupped hands. It was something ephemeral, ethereal—delicate and pure and bright. Like a tiny dragon, painted in colors too bright to see.

Hope. That's what it was. In my hand, I could almost feel its warmth, feel its glow, feel the brush of its wings. I held it there for a moment as I smiled at Colin, filled with sorrow and joy.

Then I moved my hand to my pocket and dropped it in. It's there to this day.

CHAPTER 11

LIVING IN THE BROWNS

Adventures are never fun while you're having them.

C. S. LEWIS, *The Voyage of the Dawn Treader*

I'M WRITING THIS a few days after Thanksgiving—that weird holiday stuck between the Halloween buying season and the Christmas buying season. It's about food and football and a little about faith—a time when we take stock of all our blessings. All that we have to be thankful for.

That makes it hard for some. They think about a nephew stricken with stage 4 cancer. They sit by a loved one with Alzheimer's. They stare at the empty spot at the dinner table.

Depression can make gratitude difficult to reach too. It's our very own wet blanket, constantly wet and constantly smothering. It can turn the cranberry sauce bland, the football boring, and the people—even the people you most love in the world—insufferable. Even Uncle Howard's annual rant about how lizard people have taken over the postal service can lose its appeal. Depression makes it hard to be thankful about much of anything.

So you might want to sit down for the next part: I'm thankful for my depression.

Yes, that comes with plenty of caveats. I'm aware that my own depression is not nearly as severe as what other people may suffer from. I've never needed electroconvulsive therapy or been on a cornucopia of medications. I can't speak for anyone else but me. Nor is this to say that I *like* depression, or that I *enjoy* depression, or that I really miss the days when I'd literally lie around for weeks staring at nothing, either feeling dead or wishing I was. Depression is just the worst.

But it also helped make me who I am.

Any eleven-year-old boy can tell you that scars are kinda cool. They're like horrific little bumper stickers that tell the world you've *been through stuff, man.* A cool divot down your cheek? You could've gotten that in a knife fight, by golly. That crooked little finger? MMA tournament, of course. If you wear an eyepatch, you'll never go dateless for the rest of your life. Scars tell the world (rightly or no) that you're not someone to be trifled with.

Emotional scars are, admittedly, not so cool—especially when you're a guy, and those emotional scars make you more inclined to weep during *Avengers: Endgame.* (I'm not admitting anything.) But they're still a part of us. They remind us, if no one else, that we made it through something tough and survived. Those scars speak to a part of our story. And I think sometimes the most glorious stories can be the hardest to get through.

When was there ever a great story free from drama and trauma and tragedy?

We struggle and suffer—suffer more than we'd like, certainly, because who wants to suffer at all? Not me, that's for sure. But would we ever appreciate moments of happiness if we never understood sadness? Would we appreciate the light if we'd never seen it dark? When I think about my favorite things to eat or drink, I think about doughnuts or bacon or Mountain Dew. No one would ever say *water*. Water is about as bland as it gets . . . unless you've just come in from an eight-mile run and drink a cold glass of the stuff. Not even a steak from a five-star restaurant could compare to the exquisite, sharp, fresh taste of water—the sort of sensation that goes beyond smell and taste, but hits you in the back of the throat, your chest, your fingers.

My anxiety and depression make it, I think, harder for me to feel the sort of happiness that some others feel as a matter of routine. So when I do feel joy—when I'm at ease with friends and family, when I'm at peace with myself, when I wish I could live forever and feel like I just might do it—those moments are all the more special for me. It's like that water after a run. It's the law of emotional capitalism: supply and demand. My psyche doesn't allow me as many of those moments, but when I have them, they seem all the more special to me. And honestly, sometimes I wonder if our emotional bank accounts—deposit boxes filled with all our lives' loose joy—wind up looking just about even.

Obviously, when depression's chewing on your psyche like a dog with an old tennis ball, those moments of joy can be very rare indeed, if they come at all. But I think that even when we feel incapable of free, laughing happiness, we can find a different, quieter sort of joy.

This is a hard thing to articulate, but let me try.

My family has deep Colorado roots, and they sink the deepest in its sprawling, arid San Luis Valley. My great-great-grandfather home-steaded there in 1887, just eleven years after the territory became a state. My great-grandparents raised most of their fourteen children in a tiny log cabin there. Grandpa Carl (on my Dad's side) was a farmer and fireman in Alamosa, the valley's biggest town. Grandpa Ted (on my mom's side) sold furniture there. Lots of my relatives still call the valley home, and they would not want to move anywhere else.

But none of them would likely say it's ever been an easy place to live.

When most folks outside Colorado imagine the state, they picture Aspen or Vail or Rocky Mountain National Park: green and beautiful and, well, kinda rich. I've never been to Aspen, but I'm pretty sure town officials check your credit score at the gate.

The San Luis Valley is as Colorado as it comes, but it's cold and dry and poor. Alamosa gets nine inches of rain a year, about the same as Phoenix. With temperatures drifting to 20-, 30-, or even 40-below-zero in winter, it's often colder than Fairbanks or Fargo. Poverty rates hover around 20 to 25 percent.[1] My great-great grandmother, Martha Minnesota Nelson, died just weeks after she moved there, from (according to another ancestor of mine, Nellie Patton) "the cold, high altitude."[2]

I loved visiting Alamosa when I was little. The Christmas decorations sparkled on Main Street, the old locomotive stationed in the park fueled a hundred stories. But by my sophomore year of high school—when I was most full of myself and my biggish, Colorado Springs–city ways—I didn't find Alamosa so charming. I loved my Grandma Dorothy and still enjoyed our visits, but in my tiny grandma's tiny house,* heated only by a gas-powered Franklin stove, I was growing more conscious of the relative poverty there.

That consciousness felt like it hit its apex in my sophomore

---

* She was probably all of four foot eleven, and the house couldn't have been more than 700 square feet. I think my Grandpa Carl, who'd passed away a bit before, had actually built the home's bathroom. I can still remember the old-fashioned doorknobs, and how you had to pull *hard* to get the door to actually latch the way it should.

year, when my family went down to visit my Grandma Dorothy late one fall, when Alamosa's charms felt at their lowest. It was warm for Alamosa in November . . . which meant it wasn't very. Everything was dead. And for some reason, Dad wanted to go for a walk through a vacant mile of weeds nearby.

My sister and I dutifully pulled on three or four sweaters, slapped on a stocking hat or two, wrote our wills, and dove into the sparse Alamosa air after my father. We trudged through thin, shaking brush and under the skeletal elms and cottonwoods. We poked around the trash and explored some old, metal ruins of what might've been part of an old city project or depot or burned-down insane asylum. I don't think I'd ever seen a landscape look quite so scrubby and lifeless and poor.

And just as I was thinking how ugly everything looked, my dad stopped, put his hands on his hips, and said, "Isn't this beautiful?"

Beautiful? I thought. "Beautiful?" I said.

"Yeah," Dad said. "Just look at all those browns!"

I looked at the browns and remained unimpressed, convinced my dad had finally lost it. At the time, I was pretty sure that when I became a Pulitzer Prize–winning writer, I was going to settle down in Oregon or Washington, somewhere that actually got some rain. For me, the beauty of nature was dependent on nature being green and lush. Or, at least, green. In nature, brown was the color of dirt, of grime, of dead leaves, of . . . well, other less pleasant things. Of all the colors in the average Crayola box, brown seemed like the worst color.

But now I understand.

Now, when Emily and I run through the scrub in October or February, through yellowed grass and bare trees as the wind sets them all to shivering, I sometimes say, "Look at these browns!" mimicking my dad but, truth be told, mocking myself. "Isn't it beautiful?" And we agree it is.

It *is* beautiful. It's not beautiful in the same way as a Hawaiian beach or an Oregon rain forest or a snowcapped Colorado peak, but look closely, and you'll find a subtle beauty just as rich, just as powerful. Shades and textures blend and meld, like mellow rivers of honey and earth. You see the architecture of the trees, the graceful shoot and brush of the grass, hear something rustling deep in its hidden paths. It's the sort of beauty that doesn't translate into postcards or Instagram pics, but somehow imprints itself somewhere inside you.

I've seen plenty of typically gorgeous places in this beautiful country of ours: Yosemite and its cliffs of white and green; Carlsbad's endless, shimmering stalagmites and stalactites; the Hoh Rain Forest's cool, moss-caked woods. Anyone can look at these places and see the beauty in them, even if they're fiddling with their phones. But to see the beauty in the browns requires your attention. You walk. You stop and listen for a while, to the wind carve past the twigs like a skier through trees. Listen to the branches creak and brush against each other with dry familiarity. Watch the shadows define the seeds of the grass. Feel the poke and prickle against your fingertips. Smell the earth underneath.

Depression helps you see the beauty in the browns.

Sure, it robs the color and vibrancy of your days and weeks, and as you begin to crawl out of its smothering embrace, the color returns only by inches. But as it comes back, I think—if you're willing to look—you can see texture and shadow in the folds of your life that, perhaps, you'd never have seen without it. At least that's how it feels to me. And moreover, you find comfort there. When the noise and splash and *feel* of the world grows too loud, those browns . . . the gentle creases and seams you found in the threads of your life that perhaps you discovered when you were miserable . . . are there. And you wrap yourself in them like a blanket.

There was a time in my life, when I was feeling pretty good about myself, that I stopped reading. I rediscovered books when I needed them, in the aftermath of depression, and now, as I write, I'm surrounded by them—old friends with me always, even when I feel alone. I enjoy hearing the clock tick and the refrigerator hum, listen for cars two streets down. I know nothing about cooking, but one of my favorite things to do during quiet evenings is flip on a cooking show and watch it with Wendy, still holding hands after all this time. These are the browns of life—easily overlooked but both strong and gentle, warm, comforting. The touch of bark. The scent of topsoil. The warmth of a river rock clutched in your hand.

The silence you feel from God, the separation you feel from others, and the deep, nightmarish introspection of depression are horrific. But traveling through that depression helped unlock an understanding that there are good manifestations of all those things, in moderation. When I crawl free of depression, even partly, I see that some of its most terrible elements and emotions can mellow into things that look a lot like virtues.

When I'm depressed, I *obsess*. When I'm not, that depression has given me a better ability to *reflect*. When I'm depressed, I feel worthless. But that depression has also given me the tendency to be, I think, a little more humble, a little more realistic about my own weaknesses, than I otherwise would be. I've learned the difference between being lonely and the quiet joy of being alone. I think I've learned that, sometimes, what seems like God's stony silence can really be God's quiet presence. Perhaps these things would've been a part of me without my depression. But I kind of doubt it.

Several chapters ago, I wrote about a man dying from cancer, and how he sometimes felt so alone in his prayer time. This same man had a brother who was a cancer survivor. He knew, intimately, the struggles that come with the disease. He said something that impacted me deeply.

"In the Western World, we Christians tend to pray, 'God, take this burden away from me,'" he said. "In the rest of the world, Christians are more likely to ask, 'God, give me the strength to carry this burden.'"

That's my prayer these days. Not for God to take away the static or to wipe depression clean away from me and make me "normal," but I pray for the strength, if and when it comes back, to deal with it. Because, honestly and with a deep sense of irony, I feel closer to God because of it.

It pushes me into a place of dependency. When I feel worthless and alone and weak, I understand how much I must trust in Him to carry me over and through. Like Peter told Jesus, where else would I go? No one else can save me. No one else can make me feel whole. When I'm down, I know that I have no virtue, no strength, no talent to offer. I'm a supplicant with knee bent, neck exposed, begging for grace. I have no other hope.

For the Christian world, depression is a vexing mystery. Is it borne of sin? Is it possession? Is it a lack of faith? And if it's none of those things, why did God see fit to allow this affliction to visit those who suffer from it? Why so burden the loved ones who have to deal with it in someone else? What kind of God would have us be in that sort of pain and melancholy?

In 1958, J. R. R. Tolkien wrote a letter to a person named Rhona Beare, trying to explain a point of theology behind his creative opus *Lord of the Rings* and the idea that the mortality of man, while a punishment borne of Middle Earth's version of original sin, was something else as well.

"A divine 'punishment' is also a divine 'gift,' if accepted, since its object is ultimate blessing, and the supreme inventiveness of the Creator will make 'punishments' . . . produce a good not otherwise to be attained," Tolkien wrote.[3]

In an interview with *GQ* magazine, *Late Show* host, practicing Catholic, and self-professed Tolkien geek Stephen Colbert unpacked a terrible tragedy in his own life, when his father and two of his brothers (Peter and Paul) were killed in a plane crash when Colbert was just ten. He describes how his own mother was broken but never bitter. How he learned from her example and tried, always, to make her laugh. How she drew on her faith in that terrible time, and how he learned from that, too.

"That might be why you don't see me as someone angry and working out my demons onstage," Colbert told *GQ*'s Joel Lovell. "It's that I love the thing that I most wish had not happened."[4]

And then, Colbert paraphrased Tolkien from that 1958 letter. "What punishments of God are not gifts?"

I love that. *What punishments of God are not gifts?*

Depression is a disease. It is an affliction. It, perhaps, *can* be a punishment for sins too tightly held. I hate it, and I hate what it does to me.

And yet, it can be . . . a gift.

I'm grateful for every moment of my life—every scar I've collected, every pain I've suffered. I can't imagine life without having experienced and earned them. The days I've spent in the browns I'd not trade for weeks in beauty.

Pain is a gift. Sadness is a gift. Even suffering can be a gift if we learn from it or it makes us stronger or if someone else can find a gift of his or her own drawn from our struggles. We are tools in the hand of the Almighty. And sometimes, I think our hurt—as awful as it can be—can also be an instrument of healing. When we suffer and still believe, when we doubt and yet hope, maybe we help illustrate another side of the Christian journey, one not often publicized in chipper praise music or inspirational talks or too-easy smiles on Sunday mornings, a journey walked among the browns. And maybe that hurt can help even the hurters, too.

In his second letter to the Corinthians, Paul wrote this famous passage:

> So to keep me from becoming conceited because of the surpassing greatness of the revelations, a thorn was given me in the flesh, a messenger of Satan to harass me, to keep me from becoming conceited. Three times I pleaded with the Lord about this, that it should leave me. But he said to me, "My grace is sufficient for you, for my power is made perfect in weakness." Therefore I will boast all the more gladly of my weaknesses, so that the power of Christ may rest upon me.
>
> 2 CORINTHIANS 12:7-9

I don't know what depression is for me—a thorn in the flesh, a disease, a punishment. But I believe that in my weakness, God can work. When depression makes me feel empty, perhaps God can fill me with something better.

I have no real assurances that "I'm all better now." I think depression's a little like cancer: Sometimes you have it and get rid of it, and it's gone for good. Sometimes you have it and get rid of it, and it comes back. And maybe, for a few (or more than a few), it never fully goes away. It shrinks or grows depending on myriad factors and maybe its own unfathomable timetable. As much as running and writing and friends and family and God have helped me through the days and years to stay relatively sane and relatively hopeful, I've learned that depression loves its little surprises.

But I'm not scared of it. As most directors of horror movies know—most good ones, anyway—the fear is in the unknown. But this horror, I know. I've seen the face of depression. I've heard its lies and half-truths and nihilistic whispers. And I have a better idea how to quell the rising static if and when it returns. I know how to fight it, and how you can too.

You live.

You stare depression in the eye and live. You drown its whispers with your own song. You push it away with counseling and meds and friends and family and laughter and joy whenever you can find it, in what meager doses you're allowed. You read. You run. You work. You play. You love your kids, love your parents, love your friends, love all of this glorious gift of life you can, because it is a gift—even when it doesn't feel like it. To feel the miracle in each breath, to feel creation's treasures under your touch like tiny jewels, to listen for the melody of this impossibly ancient and always renewing universe that we're a part of.

Depression tells us we're as good as dead. It's a lie. Depression tells us we're better off dead. Not when we still have so much of our story to live.

Several years ago, folks were getting tattoos of, of all things, semi-colons. You'd see them on people's wrists or ankles. It seemed to me like an odd choice for a tattoo when I first started seeing them. Most folks don't even know how to use them in an actual sentence. Why adorn your body with a bit of outdated English punctuation?

But that tiny, outdated bit of English punctuation—a dot and a comma that signifies a break in a sentence, a transition to another, related thought—tells a story of its own. Many of those who bear it thought about turning their lives into a complete sentence—putting a period on their existences and closing the book. *Over. Done. Dead.* Instead, they kept going; they decided to go on, just as a semicolon allows a sentence to go on.

I'd encourage that use of our life's semicolons—to go on, leaning as we do into faith, and hope, and love. We embrace faith even when we can't hear God; we insist on hoping even when things feel hopeless. We love even when we're sure we're unlovable. Our will is a testament to them all. And that will is not a feeling, it is an action, a decision, a statement of power. We believe, we hope, we love because we choose to. We *choose.*

We live. Because no night lasts forever. Light and warmth lies just east of here, on the horizon. It's there. If you wait, you may see its glimmer, out there in the gloom.

But in the meantime, like Dante, look up, too. Look up and see the stars. Look up and see the sky, spreading so vast and broad and deep. Look up and see its Author, and yours. Trust Him to finish your story.

I can't promise you will be without pain, without suffering, without confusion and doubt.

But it'll be a story worth reading. Of that I am sure.

NOTES

CHAPTER 1: HIDDEN

1. Bradford Richardson, "Religious People More Likely to Give to Charity, Study Shows," *Washington Times*, October 30, 2017, https://www.washingtontimes .com/news/2017/oct/30/religious-people-more-likely-give-charity-study/.
2. Jonathan Edwards, *Sinners in the Hands of an Angry God,* https://www .goodreads.com/quotes/890641-the-devil-stands-waiting-for-them-like -greedy-hungry-lions.
3. C. S. Lewis, *Mere Christianity*, C. S. Lewis Institute website, https://www .cslewisinstitute.org/webfm_send/4509.
4. Charlotte Donlon, "My Pastor Told Me It Was a Sin Not to Feel Joy. Here's What Happens When Churches Ignore Mental Illness," *Washington Post*, September 26, 2016, https://www.washingtonpost.com/news/acts-of-faith /wp/2016/09/26/my-pastor-told-me-it-was-a-sin-not-to-feel-joy-heres-what -happens-when-churches-ignore-mental-illness/.
5. Michael Foust, "Study Finds Religious People Less Likely than Atheists to Be Depressed When Lonely," *Christian Headlines,* September 6, 2018, https:// www.christianheadlines.com/contributors/michael-foust/study-finds-religious -people-less-likely-than-atheists-to-be-depressed-when-lonely.html.
6. Lisa Miller et al., "Religiosity and Major Depression in Adults at High Risk: A Ten-Year Prospective Study," *American Journal of Psychiatry* 169, no. 1 (January 2012): 89–94, https://www.ncbi.nlm.nih.gov/pmc/articles/PMC3547523/.
7. Kanita Dervic et al., "Religious Affiliation and Suicide Attempt," *American Journal of Psychiatry* 161, no. 12 (December 2004): https://ajp .psychiatryonline.org/doi/10.1176/appi.ajp.161.12.2303.
8. Rick Warren, interview by Piers Morgan, *Piers Morgan Live*, CNN, September 17, 2013, http://transcripts.cnn.com/TRANSCRIPTS/1309/17/pmt.01.html.
9. "Rick Warren Returns to Pulpit 16 Weeks After Son's Death," CBS Los Angeles, July 27, 2013, https://losangeles.cbslocal.com/2013/07/27/pastor -rick-warren-returns-to-pulpit-after-16-weeks/.
10. Ed Stetzer, "Suicide, Mental Illness, and the Church: An Interview with Kay Warren," *Christianity Today*, October 11, 2017, https://www.christianitytoday .com/edstetzer/2017/october/suicide-mental-illness-and-church-interview -with-kay-warren.html.

11. Kay Warren, Facebook, December 15, 2015, https://www.facebook.com
/105128507568/posts/when-i-wrote-choose-joy-because-happiness-isnt
-enough-i-revealed-that-i-had-a-cl/10153346150127569/.
12. N. T. Wright, *Paul: A Biography* (San Francisco: HarperOne, 2018), 45.
13. Wright, 45.

CHAPTER 2: WHAT IS DEPRESSION?

1. Wikipedia, s.v. "List of Colorado Fourteeners," last modified May 26, 2020,
21:09, https://en.wikipedia.org/wiki/List_of_Colorado_fourteeners.
2. Colorado.com staff writer, "What Are 14ers?" *Colorado.com*, July 8, 2020,
https://www.colorado.com/articles/what-are-14ers.
3. Josh Friesema, "How Many 14ers Are in Colorado?" *OutThere Colorado*, July
10, 2019, https://www.outtherecolorado.com/52-fourteeners-in-colorado
-or-is-it-74-well/.
4. "Sleep and Mental Health," *Harvard Mental Health Letter*, Harvard Health
Publishing, July 2009, https://www.health.harvard.edu/newsletter_article
/sleep-and-mental-health.
5. "Depression," World Health Organization (fact sheet), January 30, 2020,
https://www.who.int/news-room/fact-sheets/detail/depression.
6. Marilee Hanson, "John Keats, Letters to Benjamin Bailey, 21,25 May 1818,"
https://englishhistory.net/keats/letters/benjamin-bailey-2125-may-1818/.
7. Andrew Solomon, *The Noonday Demon: An Atlas of Depression* (New York:
Scribner, 2002).
8. Dick Cavett, quoted in Nikki Martinez, "230 Depression Quotes on Mental
Health to Help You Feel Understood," *Everyday Power*, March 27, 2020,
https://everydaypower.com/depression-quotes/.
9. Solomon, 16.
10. "What Causes Depression?" Harvard Health Publishing, June 2009, https://
www.health.harvard.edu/mind-and-mood/what-causes-depression.
11. "What Causes Depression?"
12. Douglas F. Levinson and Walter E. Nichols, "Major Depression and Genetics,"
Genetics of Brain Function, Stanford Medicine, http://med.stanford.edu
/depressiongenetics/mddandgenes.html.
13. Solomon, 67.
14. Daniel Hass, "This Is How the Brain Filters Out Unimportant Details,"
Psychology Today, February 11, 2015, https://www.psychologytoday.com/us
/blog/brain-babble/201502/is-how-the-brain-filters-out-unimportant-details.
15. Maggie Fox, "Major Depression on the Rise Among Everyone, New Data
Shows," NBC News, May 10, 2018, https://www.nbcnews.com/health/health
-news/major-depression-rise-among-everyone-new-data-shows-n873146.
16. Tammy Worth, "10 Careers wth High Rates of Depression," Health.com,
February 26, 2011, https://www.health.com/condition/depression/10
-careers-with-high-rates-of-depression.
17. Worth, "10 Careers."

18. "Mental Health by the Numbers," National Alliance on Mental Illness, September 2019, https://www.nami.org/Learn-More/Mental-Health-By -the-Numbers.

19. "Suicide" fact sheet, CDC.gov, 2015, https://www.cdc.gov/violenceprevention /pdf/suicide-datasheet-a.pdf.

20. "Why People Get Happier as They Get Older," *The Economist*, December 23, 2016, https://medium.economist.com/why-people-get-happier-as-they-get -older-b5e412e471ed.

21. "Depression in the Elderly," WebMD, https://www.webmd.com/depression /guide/depression-elderly#1.

22. Janice C. Probst et al., "Rural-Urban Differences in Depression Prevalence: Implications for Family Medicine," *Family Medicine* 38, no. 9, October 2006, https://fammedarchives.blob.core.windows.net/imagesandpdfs/fmhub /fm2006/October/Janice653.pdf.

23. David Levine, "Can Where You Live Affect Your Depression Risk?" *U.S. News & World Report*, May 8, 2017, https://health.usnews.com/health-care/patient -advice/articles/2017-05-08/can-where-you-live-affect-your-depression-risk.

24. Matt Wray et al., "Leaving Las Vegas: Exposure to Las Vegas and Risk of Suicide," *Social Science & Medicine*, December 2008, https://www .sciencedirect.com/science/article/abs/pii/S0277953608004425.

25. Ken Alltucker and Lilly Price, "Suicide Rates—a State by State Look," *USA Today*, December 13, 2018, https://www.usatoday.com/list/news/depression -suicide-by-state/346e182d-d439-4448-b8d9-a0233a45f598/.

26. David Railton, "How High Altitudes Could Raise Risk of Depression, Suicide," *Medical News Today*, March 16, 2018, https://www .medicalnewstoday.com/articles/321219.

CHAPTER 3: BELONGING

1. "What's It Like in the Womb?" WebMD.com, https://www.webmd.com /baby/features/in-the-womb#1.

2. Erich Fromm, *The Art of Loving: The Centennial Edition* (New York: Bloomsbury Academic, 2000), 9.

3. Adam Cash, "Psychologist Sigmund Freud's Stages of Sexual Development," dummies.com, https://www.dummies.com/education/psychology /psychologist-sigmund-freuds-stages-of-sexual-development/.

4. "Cognitive and Social Skills to Expect from 6 to 10 Years," American Psychological Association, ACT Raising Safe Kids Program fact sheet, June 2017, https://www.apa.org/act/resources/fact-sheets/development-10-years.

5. Larry Cuban, "The Open Classroom," *Education Next* 4, no. 2 (Spring 2004), https://www.educationnext.org/theopenclassroom/.

6. "Student Reports of Bullying: Results from the 2015 School Crime Supplement to the National Crime Victimization Survey," U.S. Department of Education (December 2016), Table 2:1, https://nces.ed.gov/pubs2017 /2017015.pdf.

7. William E. Copeland et al., "Adult Psychiatric and Suicide Outcomes of Bullying and Being Bullied by Peers in Childhood and Adolescence," *JAMA Psychiatry* 70, no. 4 (April 1, 2013): 419–26, https://www.ncbi.nlm.nih.gov /pmc/articles/PMC3618584/.

8. Mark Ellis, "Victims of Bullying Most Likely to Become Bullies Themselves," *The Mirror*, April 19, 2016, https://www.mirror.co.uk/news/uk-news/victims -bullying-most-likely-become-7785034.

9. Craig Timberg, "Many Teens Sleep With Their Phones, Survey Finds—Just Like Their Parents," *Washington Post*, May 28, 2019, https://www .washingtonpost.com/business/technology/mimicking-their-parents-many -teens-sleep-with-their-phones-survey-finds/2019/05/28/1bf2ee68-8188 -11e9-9a67-a687ca99fb3d_story.html?noredirect=on.

10. "Nationwide Teen Bullying and Cyberbullying Study Reveals Significant Issues Impacting Youth," *Science Daily*, February 21, 2017, https://www .sciencedaily.com/releases/2017/02/170221102036.htm.

11. Raychelle Cassada Lohmann, "What's Driving the Rise in Teen Depression?" *U.S. News & World Report*, April 22, 2019, https://health.usnews.com /wellness/for-parents/articles/2019-04-22/teen-depression-is-on-the-rise.

CHAPTER 4: OF BRAIN AND BLOOD

1. "Data and Statistics on Children's Mental Health," Centers for Disease Control and Prevention, March 30, 2020, https://www.cdc.gov /childrensmentalhealth/data.html.

2. Craig N. Sawchuk, "Is It Possible to Have Depression and Anxiety at the Same Time?" Mayo Clinic, June 2, 2017, https://www.mayoclinic.org /diseases-conditions/depression/expert-answers/depression-and-anxiety /faq-20057989.

3. "Facts and Statistics," Anxiety and Depression Association of America, https:// adaa.org/about-adaa/press-room/facts-statistics.

4. Mayo Clinic Staff, "Teen Depression," Mayo Clinic, https://www.mayoclinic .org/diseases-conditions/teen-depression/symptoms-causes/syc-20350985.

5. Therese J. Borchard, "Why Are So Many Teens Depressed?" *Psych Central*, July 8, 2018, https://psychcentral.com/blog/why-are-so-many-teens-depressed/.

6. Melissa Healy, "Suicide Rates for U.S. Teens and Young Adults Are the Highest on Record," *Los Angeles Times*, June 18, 2019, https://www.latimes.com /science/la-sci-suicide-rates-rising-teens-young-adults-20190618-story.html.

7. "Youth Suicide Statistics," The Parent Resource Program from The Jason Foundation, http://prp.jasonfoundation.com/facts/youth-suicide-statistics/.

8. Brad Underwood, "Ohio Dept. of Health Says Suicide Is the Leading Cause of Death in Kids Aged 10-14," Local 12, November 20, 2019, https://local12 .com/news/local/ohio-dept-of-health-says-suicide-is-the-leading-cause-of -death-in-kids-aged-10-14.

9. "9-year-old Girl Commits Suicide after Months of Being Bullied at Her

School," *Atlanta Voice*, September 25, 2019, https://www.theatlantavoice
.com/articles/9-year-old-girl-commits-suicide-after-months-of-being-bullied
-at-her-school/.

10. "Health Consequences of Drug Misuse: Mental Health Effects," National
Institute on Drug Abuse, March 2017, https://www.drugabuse.gov
/publications/health-consequences-drug-misuse/mental-health-effects.

11. "Mental Disorders and Drug Abuse in Teens," Addiction Center, December 6,
2019, https://www.addictioncenter.com/teenage-drug-abuse/co-occurring
-disorders/.

12. Antoine de Saint-Exupéry, *The Little Prince* (New York: Reynal & Hitchcock,
1943), 42–43.

13. Andrew Solomon, *The Noonday Demon* (New York: Scribner, 2014), 39.

14. Ashley Tripp, "Why Students Lose Their Faith in College," Cru, https://www
.cru.org/us/en/communities/campus/why-students-lose-faith-in-college.html.

15. Jeanie Lerche Davis, "Cutting and Self-Harm: Warning Signs and Treatment,"
WebMD, https://www.webmd.com/mental-health/features/cutting-self-harm
-signs-treatment#1.

16. Davis, "Cutting and Self-Harm."

17. D'Arcy Lyness, "Cutting," *TeensHealth from Nemours*, July 2015, https://
kidshealth.org/en/teens/cutting.html.

18. Davis, "Cutting and Self-Harm."

19. "Depression," Mental Health America, https://www.mhanational.org
/conditions/depression.

20. Erich Fromm, *The Art of Loving* (New York: Bantam, 1963), 47.

CHAPTER 5: GUT CHECK

1. Amy Smith, "What Are the Early Signs of a Depression Relapse?," *Medical
News Today*, August 20, 2019, https://www.medicalnewstoday.com/articles
/320269.

2. Jürgen Unützer and Mijung Park, "Strategies to Improve the Management
of Depression in Primary Care," *Primary Care* 39, no. 2, June 2012, https://
www.ncbi.nlm.nih.gov/pmc/articles/PMC4127627/.

3. "Understanding Depression Relapses and Why They Occur," Pyramid Healthcare,
June 4, 2019, https://www.pyramidhealthcarepa.com/depression-relapses/.

4. "Famous Last Words: Notable Suicide Notes," phrases.org, https://www
.phrases.org.uk/famous-last-words//suicide-notes.html.

5. Burkhard Bilger, "The Ride of Their Lives," *New Yorker*, December 1, 2014,
https://www.newyorker.com/magazine/2014/12/08/ride-lives.

CHAPTER 6: SILENCE

1. George Graham, "Unwholly Bound: Mother Teresa's Battles with Depression,"
Oxford University Press blog, April 13, 2016, https://blog.oup.com/2016/04
/mother-teresa-depression/.

2. Brian Kolodiejchuk, ed., *Mother Teresa: Come Be My Light: The Private Writings of the Saint of Calcutta* (London: Ebury Publishing, 2003), 192.

3. "In the U.S., Decline of Christianity Continues at Rapid Pace," Pew Research Center, October 17, 2019, https://www.pewforum.org/2019/10/17/in-u-s -decline-of-christianity-continues-at-rapid-pace/.

4. Brianna Abbott, "Youth Suicide Rate Increased 56% in Decade, CDC Says," *Wall Street Journal*, October 17, 2019, https://www.wsj.com/articles /youth-suicide-rate-rises-56-in-decade-cdc-says-11571284861.

5. Abbott, "Youth Suicide Rate."

6. Dennis Thompson, "More American Young People Are Dying by Suicide and Homicide, CDC Reports," CBS News, October 17, 2019, https://www .cbsnews.com/news/suicide-rate-homicides-rise-american-teens-youth-cdc -reports/.

7. Ashley Welch, "Depression, Anxiety, Suicide Increase in Teens and Young Adults, Study Finds," CBS News, March 14, 2019, https://www.cbsnews.com/news /suicide-depression-anxiety-mental-health-issues-increase-teens-young-adults/.

8. Rachael Rettner, "God Help Us? How Religion Is Good (and Bad) for Mental Health," *Live Science*, September 23, 2015, https://www.livescience.com/52197 -religion-mental-health-brain.html.

9. Raphael Bonelli et al., "Religious and Spiritual Factors in Depression: Review and Integration of the Research," *Depression Research and Treatment*, August 15, 2012, https://www.ncbi.nlm.nih.gov/pmc/articles/PMC3426191/.

10. Bonelli et al., "Religious and Spiritual Factors."

11. Stephen H. Webb, "God of the Depressed," *First Things*, February 19, 2016, https://www.firstthings.com/web-exclusives/2016/02/god-of-the-depressed.

12. Andrew Solomon, *The Noonday Demon* (New York: Scribner, 2014), 15.

13. "Albert Barnes' Notes on the Whole Bible: Job 2," StudyLight.org, https:// www.studylight.org/commentaries/bnb/job-2.html.

14. Annie Dillard, *Pilgrim at Tinker Creek* (New York: Harper's Magazine Press, 1970), 259.

15. David Macintosh, "Plato: A Theory of Forms," *Philosophy Now*, https:// philosophynow.org/issues/90/Plato_A_Theory_of_Forms.

16. Holmes Rolston, "Midbar, Arabah and Eremos—Biblical Wilderness," Environment & Society Portal, http://www.environmentandsociety.org /exhibitions/wilderness/midbar-arabah-and-eremos-biblical-wilderness.

17. Rabbi Joel Rembaum, "The Secret of the Yamim Nora'im: The Sound of Thin Silence," Temple Israel, October 3, 2014, http://www.tisharon.org/dvar-torah -blog/2016/1/7/the-secret-of-the-yamim-noraim-the-sound-of-thin-silence -yom-kippur-2014.

18. "The Sound of Thin Silence," Jerusalem Prayer Team, https://hebrew .jerusalemprayerteam.org/sound-thin-silence/.

19. J. R. R. Tolkien, "Letter 156," November 4, 1954, from Tolkien Gateway, http://tolkiengateway.net/wiki/Letter_156.

CHAPTER 7: ONE FOOT IN FRONT OF THE OTHER

1. Lynette L. Craft and Frank M. Perna, "The Benefits of Exercise for the Clinically Depressed," *Primary Care Companion* 6, no. 3 (2004): 104–11, https://www.ncbi.nlm.nih.gov/pmc/articles/PMC474733/.

2. "Exercise Is an All-Natural Treatment to Fight Depression," *Harvard Health Letter*, Harvard Health Publishing, July 2013 (updated March 25, 2019), https://www.health.harvard.edu/mind-and-mood/exercise-is-an-all-natural -treatment-to-fight-depression.

3. Judy Lavelle, "New Brain Effects behind 'Runner's High'," *Scientific American*, Chemical & Engineering News, October 8, 2015, https://www .scientificamerican.com/article/new-brain-effects-behind-runner-s-high/.

4. "Exercise Is an All-Natural Treatment to Fight Depression."

5. M. N. Silverman and P. A. Deuster, "Biological Mechanisms Underlying the Role of Physical Fitness in Health and Resilience," *Interface Focus* 4, no. 5 (October 6, 2014), https://www.ncbi.nlm.nih.gov/pubmed/25285199/.

6. Qing Li, "Effect of Forest Bathing Trips on Human Immune Function," *Environmental Health and Preventive Medicine* 15, no. 1 (January 2010): 9–17, https://www.ncbi.nlm.nih.gov/pmc/articles/PMC2793341/.

7. Marc G. Berman et al., "Interacting with Nature Improves Cognition and Affect for Individuals with Depression," *Journal of Affective Disorders* 140, no. 3 (November 2012): 300–305, https://www.ncbi.nlm.nih.gov/pmc /articles/PMC3393816/.

8. Rob Jordan, "Stanford Researchers Find Mental Health Prescription: Nature," *Stanford News*, June 30, 2015, https://news.stanford.edu/2015/06/30/hiking -mental-health-063015/.

9. Tom DiChiara, "Is the 'Runner's Wall' a Real Thing?" WebMD, https://www .webmd.com/fitness-exercise/features/is-the-runners-wall-a-real-thing#1.

10. Anne Lamott, *Bird by Bird* (New York: Random House, 1995), 19.

CHAPTER 8: A TIME FOR EVERYTHING

1. "Abraham Lincoln.; The Characteristics of His Life as Seen by His Law Partner," *New York Times* archives, December 31, 1865, https://www.nytimes .com/1865/12/31/archives/abraham-lincoln-the-characteristics-of-his-life-as -seen-by-his-law.html.

2. William Hanchett, *Out of the Wilderness: The Life of Abraham Lincoln* (Champaign, Illinois: University of Illinois Press, 1994), 136.

3. Doris Kearns Goodwin, *Team of Rivals: The Political Genius of Abraham Lincoln* (Champaign, IL: University of Illinois Press, 1994), 99.

4. Michael Burlingame, *Abraham Lincoln: A Life, Volume 1* (Baltimore: The Johns Hopkins University Press, 2008), 101.

5. Burlingame, 101.

6. Goodwin, 99.

7. Goodwin, 99.

8. Goodwin, 100.

9. Jacqueline Mitchell, "Mental Illness Affects Us All," Tufts Now, February 28, 2014, https://now.tufts.edu/articles/mental-illness-affects-us-all.

10. "Facts and Statistics," Anxiety and Depression Association of America, https://adaa.org/about-adaa/press-room/facts-statistics.

11. "Mental Health in the Workplace," World Health Organization, May 2019, https://www.who.int/mental_health/in_the_workplace/en/.

12. Ulysses S. Grant fact sheet, Ulysses S. Grant National Historic Site, National Park Service, https://www.nps.gov/ulsg/learn/historyculture/ulysses-s -grant.htm.

13. "Sherman, Grant, and Depression," *The Rambling Intellectual* (blog), May 1, 2016, https://theramblingintellectual.wordpress.com/2016/05/01/sherman -grant-and-depression/.

14. Linus Pierpont Brockett, *Our Great Captains: Grant, Sherman, Thomas, Sheridan, and Farragut* (New York: C. B. Richardson, 1865), 162.

15. "A Point of View: Churchill, Chance and the 'Black Dog,'" *BBC News Magazine*, September 23, 2011, https://www.bbc.com/news/magazine -15033046.

16. Carol Breckenridge, "Leading Churchill Myths—The Myth of the 'Black Dog,'" *Finest Hour* 155 (International Churchill Society), Summer 2012, https://winstonchurchill.org/publications/finest-hour/finest-hour-155/the -myth-of-the-black-dog/.

17. David L. Lewis, Clayborne Carson, "Martin Luther King, Jr.," *Encyclopaedia Britannica*, updated March 31, 2020, https://www.britannica.com/biography /Martin-Luther-King-Jr.

18. Nassir Ghaemi, "Martin Luther King: Depressed and Creatively Maladjusted," *Psychology Today*, January 16, 2012, https://www.psychologytoday.com/us /blog/mood-swings/201201/martin-luther-king-depressed-and-creatively -maladjusted.

19. Karen E. James, "From Mohandas to Mahatma: The Spiritual Metamorphosis of Gandhi," *Essays in History*, Corcoran Department of History at the University of Virginia, vol. 28 (1984): 5–20, http://www.lib.virginia.edu/area -studies/SouthAsia/gandhi.html.

20. Erich J. Prince, "Interview with Nassir Ghaemi: Can Mental Illness Make More Effective Politicians?" *Merion West*, November 17, 2018, https:// merionwest.com/2018/11/17/interview-with-nassir-ghaemi-can-mental -illness-make-more-effective-politicians/.

21. Peter Kreeft, *Back to Virtue: Traditional Moral Wisdom for Modern Moral Confusion* (San Francisco: Ignatius Press, 1992). (Italics in the original.)

22. Dante Alighieri, "Inferno, Canto I," trans. Henry Wadsworth Longfellow, https://poets.org/poem/inferno-canto-i.

23. Dante Alighieri, "The Inferno," trans. John Ciardi (New York: New American Library, 1954).

24. Dante, "Inferno," trans. Longfellow.

CHAPTER 9: DARK NIGHT

1. Douglas Adams, *The Hitchhiker's Guide to the Galaxy* (London: Pan Books, 1979), 25.

2. C. S. Lewis, *The Silver Chair* (New York: Harper Collins, 1953), 181–82. (Italics in the original.)

3. Julia Baird, "Doubt as a Sign of Faith," *New York Times*, September 25, 2014, https://www.nytimes.com/2014/09/26/opinion/julia-baird-doubt-as-a-sign-of-faith.html.

4. C. S. Lewis, *Mere Christianity* from *The Complete C. S. Lewis Signature Classics* collection (New York: HarperOne, 1952), 78.

5. M. J. Friedrich, "Depression Is the Leading Cause of Disability Around the World," *JAMA*, April 18, 2017, https://jamanetwork.com/journals/jama/article-abstract/2618635.

6. Susan J. Noonan, "Volunteer When Depressed? The Life You Save May Be Your Own," *Psychology Today*, June 18, 2016, https://www.psychologytoday.com/us/blog/view-the-mist/201606/volunteer-when-depressed-the-life-you-save-may-be-your-own.

7. Kaleigh Rogers, "Volunteering Is the Best Kept Secret for Mental Health," *Vice*, December 5, 2017, https://www.vice.com/en_us/article/a37nvk/volunteering-is-the-best-kept-secret-for-mental-health-stressweek2017.

8. Jessica Pigg, "Theology of a Red Door," Biblical Woman, August 11, 2015, https://biblicalwoman.com/red-door/.

9. Brian W. Thomas, "Font to Table: Why Do So Many Churches Have Red Doors?" 1517.org, January 22, 2019, https://www.1517.org/articles/font-to-table-why-do-so-many-churches-have-red-doors.

10. Eric Weiner, "Where Heaven and Earth Come Closer," *New York Times*, March 9, 2012, https://www.nytimes.com/2012/03/11/travel/thin-places-where-we-are-jolted-out-of-old-ways-of-seeing-the-world.html.

CHAPTER 10: THE DRAGON

1. William Shakespeare, *As You Like It*, act 3, scene 2.

2. Charles Swindoll, *The Grace Awakening* (Nashville: Thomas Nelson, 2006).

CHAPTER 11: LIVING IN THE BROWNS

1. Ted Conover, "The Last Frontier," *Harper's Magazine*, August 2019, https://harpers.org/archive/2019/08/the-last-frontier/.

2. Nellie Patton, "The Early Days of Mosca," 1941, from a family book, *Roots & Branches of the Harry Asay Family*, ed. Harold Asay.

3. J. R. R. Tolkien, Letter 212 to Rhona Beare, 1958, tolkienestate.com, https://www.tolkienestate.com/en/writing/letters/letter-rhona-beare.html.

4. Joel Lovell, "The Late, Great Stephen Colbert," *GQ*, August 17, 2015, https://www.gq.com/story/stephen-colbert-gq-cover-story.

ABOUT THE AUTHOR

PAUL ASAY is the author of two previous books (*God on the Streets of Gotham* and *Burning Bush 2.0: How Pop Culture Replaced the Prophet*) and has coauthored several more. He has also partnered with Focus on the Family president Jim Daly on a pair of books.

He currently works in Focus on the Family's Plugged In division, reviewing movies and television shows and analyzing culture from a Christian perspective for a monthly audience that exceeds one million readers. He also freelances extensively, writing regularly for the Aleteia and Patheos websites, and he's been published by such outlets as *Time*, the *Washington Post*, and *Christianity Today*. Paul has also written for *Christian Counseling Today*, tackling subjects like cyberbullying and suicide. He's won several awards for his writing, both at Plugged In and as a secular religion reporter for *The Gazette* in Colorado Springs.